KT-388-874

# LONGMAN KEY SKILLS

## LEVEL 3

## COMMUNICATION

## Series editor: Barry Smith

Longman

**Longman Key Skills**
*titles available in the series*

Application of Number Level 1+2
Application of Number Level 3

Communication Level 1+2
Communication Level 3

Information Technology Level 1+2
Information Technology Level 3

**Pearson Education Limited**
Edinburgh Gate, Harlow
Essex CM20 2JE, England
and Associated Companies throughout the world

© DB associates 2000

The right of DB associates to be identified as authors of this work has been asserted by them in accordance with the Copyright, Designs and Patents Act 1988

All rights reserved; no part of this publication may be reproduced, stored in any retrieval system, or transmitted in any form or by any means, electronic, mechanical, photocopying, recording, or otherwise without either the prior written permission of the Publishers or a licence permitting restricted copying in the United Kingdom issued by the Copyright Licensing Agency Ltd, 90 Tottenham Court Road, London W1P 0LP.

First published 2000

**British Library Cataloguing in Publication Data**
A catalogue entry for this title is available from the British Library

ISBN 0-582-42485-2

Set by 3 in Sabon and Quay Sans
Printed in Great Britain by Henry Ling Ltd,
at the Dorset Press, Dorchester

# Contents

# How to use this book

This book helps you obtain the key skill called Communication level 3. You will be doing your key skills with your other studies in a school, college or at work. The common combinations are:

A-level and key skills
Vocational A-level and key skills

A communication key skill is not asking you to be an expert writer, public speaker or debater. It is about helping you communicate information to other people by writing and talking, and about helping you to understand information and messages written and spoken by other people. The key skill is a simple way of describing all the different skills you use when you speak or listen, read or write.

Communication is often confused with literacy. However, literacy is only about reading and writing; communication includes speaking and listening skills too.

The good news about gaining any of the key skills is that you don't always need to do extra work. The evidence for the key skill is produced while you are doing your normal study and work such as in the classroom, laboratory, workshop, or while working at a job.

Of course there is a certain cunning in knowing which of your work to keep and how to show it, and that's what this book is about. There are special sections for all popular A-level and Vocational A-level subjects which tell you exactly what you need to do.

You can use this book in different ways; it depends on what you need. For example, you might not need to read it from the beginning. To get the most out of this book, have a look at the following summary of how it is organised and decide how you can use it best.

The GNVQ Advanced awards are now called **Vocational A-levels**

From September 2001 GNVQ Foundation and Intermediate awards are likely to be known as **Vocational GCSEs**.

## Part 1: The Learning Curve

This part of the book concentrates on what you need to know to get the key skill units. It has useful information about how to participate in discussions, give a short presentation, find and read written information, and create different types of written documents.

## Part 2: The Bottom Line

This part of the book tells you what you must do to gain the key skills units. It explains:

- The words and ideas of the key skills
- The definition of level 3
- How you can practise the skills
- What must be in your portfolio of evidence

Your collection of evidence or portfolio is the key to getting your key skill. This part of the book tells you how to choose your evidence and get it ready.

## Part 3: Opportunities

This part of the book tells you where to find opportunities for evidence in the study or work you are already doing. If you are at school or college, you should look up the pages for your particular subjects at A-level or Vocational A-Level.

## Margin

Look in the margin for simple explanations of important words and ideas and for references to other places in the book where there is useful information.

# Part 1: The Learning Curve

This part concentrates on what you need to know to get your key skills qualification. It will show you what you should consider when you:

- Take part in one-to-one discussions.
- Take part in group discussions.
- Give a short talk about a subject.
- Read and understand written information.
- Write documents.

This part is divided into six sections:

- **Taking part in discussions**
- **Making a presentation**
- **Non-verbal communication**
- **Reading and synthesising information**
- **Writing documents**
- **Making yourself clear**

# Taking part in discussions

The key skill will help you learn how to take part in discussions and to participate even when you are not talking. The way you are seated and the way you are listening can create an atmosphere that encourages others to express themselves. You already discuss topics with friends, family and colleagues; this part of the key skill tries to help you develop these abilities so you can take part in discussions with any group of people.

## Contributing your ideas

In an ideal group situation everyone would want to participate and everyone would get the chance, all the contributions would be useful and relevant, and the discussion would be a worthwhile experience for everybody. Real discussions are seldom like that, but by working on the key skill you can help them to come closer.

During a discussion you may find that some people talk far more than others, maybe they dominate the exchanges, some people make irrelevant contributions or wander off the point, and some people may say nothing or very little. By thinking about your own role, you already begin to improve the quality of the discussion. You can make the discussion better for you and better for others.

Think about how you behave in the group. Remember that the group will gain more if everyone makes a contribution. This is especially important if the group needs people's reactions to an idea or a set of results. Do not make long speeches; allow others to make contributions and do not interrupt them, otherwise you won't meet the key skill requirements. Nor will you meet them if you just show up and sit quietly.

### Types of contribution

There are several ways to make a contribution:

- Making a point
- Expressing an opinion
- Explaining something
- Describing events
- Asking a question

- Answering a question
- Sharing some results

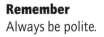

You will be assessed to see if you know how to participate appropriately, e.g. by making the right contribution at the right time or by making contributions that suit the situation. Concentrate on making an appropriate contribution each time you speak. Don't just make one contribution then keep quiet; get involved in the discussion. When you do make a contribution, show that you can adapt what you say to meet the needs of the group and the situation. For example, show you can recognise whether the discussion is formal or informal and act accordingly. Always be polite.

**Remember**
Always be polite.

# Group discussions

Create a discussion group from people you are comfortable with; discuss a topic that will interest the group. During the discussion take brief notes of key points, important decisions and who said what. They may help you to make your contribution. If you attribute an idea or comment to someone, make sure you name the right person. Done well it can be a compliment, but done badly it can lead to unnecessary arguments. The notes you take can provide a useful record of your involvement.

Perhaps begin by jotting down the names of the people taking part or even a rough seating arrangement. This will help you to identify who's who. Keep your notes brief; spend most of your time looking at the speakers not at your notepad. Eye contact is important.

**Discussion group**

Joanne    Dave

Me    Niki

Yvonne    Louise

Mark

## *Always*
- Be aware of your surroundings
- Be aware of other group members
- Be polite and supportive
- Speak clearly when you contribute
- Wait for people to finish speaking

## *Never*
- Shout or raise your voice
- Be rude or angry
- Dominate the discussion
- Decline to participate

---

### GET INVOLVED IN DISCUSSIONS

Try to get involved in discussions with small groups of people, perhaps between 4 and 6, and focus on shared interests. A shared interest might be an assignment or investigation you are all working on, or it might be an issue that interests you all. Topics that make for good discussions normally involve problems that need solving, issues that need to be debated or resolved, and questions that must be answered.

# Awareness of others

## Active listening

Even when you are not talking, there's still work to be done.

See also: **Non-verbal communication**, page 15.

**Attentive:** alert, careful, observant, having regard for others.

The point of a discussion is to exchange information and ideas with others; this means giving and receiving. The simplest way to show someone that you are listening is to look at them. You can also jot down the points they make, especially those you think are important.

There is a difference between hearing someone's voice and listening to what they are saying. It can be very off-putting to realise that people are not listening. The speaker sees the signs in glazed eyeballs, stifled yawns and perhaps even more obvious displays. And the message comes across: I'm not interested in what you're saying; I'm only interested when I'm talking. So be attentive and make sure that you really do listen to people.

Being attentive is what typifies a good listener. It means using different listening techniques to let others know you are taking an interest in what is being said. The following table shows a range of techniques to indicate you are paying attention, and you may be surprised how effective they are. But just imagine how you would feel if no one looked at you when you spoke. In fact, not looking at someone can be a sign that you aren't impressed by what they have to say.

| Listening technique | How to use it |
| --- | --- |
| Facial expressions | Give clues on how you are receiving someone<br>Puzzled looks can encourage them to explain |
| Body movements | Nodding in agreement can be encouraging<br>Shaking your head is good if you time it well<br>Tilting your head shows you are listening<br>Crossed arms look defensive<br>Open palms add emphasis |
| Asking questions | Base your questions on what people have said<br>What did you mean when you said … ?<br>You mentioned …. Can you explain it to me? |
| Verbal encouragement | Offer an occasional word or nod of approval<br>Try something like yip, uh huh, mmm (these are called affirmative verbal sounds) |

**Affirmative verbal sounds**
Noises of agreements or understanding you make during conversation.

## AN EXPERIMENT ON VERBAL ENCOURAGEMENT

Try this exercise to investigate the importance that speakers attach to verbal encouragement or reassurance. When a chatty person telephones you and starts to tell you something at length, make sure you keep quiet and say nothing. Don't even grunt or say yeh; just say nothing at all. See what kind of reaction you get. They will probably find it disconcerting and keep checking that you are there. Most telephone speakers expect their listeners to give them an occasional sound of reassurance.

When you are not under the spotlight and are in a normal conversation with a friend or a family member, you are probably highly accomplished at using these gestures. What you might need to practise is your ability to use them during your key skills assessment without being shy or inhibited.

### Understanding the facts

To test that you understand what someone has told you, repeat it back to them in your own words. It should then be clear that you have understood what was said; if you haven't understood, the other person should be able to re-explain. You can also use follow-up questions to check your understanding, or simply ask the other person to explain the whole thing in a different way.

# Asking questions and responding to others

## Questions and answers

The key skill is looking for two things:

- Whether you can listen and respond appropriately
- Whether you can use questions to encourage others

It does not expect you to have all the answers nor is it trying to see how cleverly you can avoid answering people. If you don't know something, there are three things you can do:

- Admit that you don't know
- Say how you could find out
- Ask if anyone else knows

It is important to realise the limits of your knowledge, and it is often the first step towards expanding them.

When you do answer a question, there are three things to remember:

- Use the questioner's name in your answer
- Repeat the question before you give the answer
- Do not humiliate anyone during your answer

Repeating the question before giving the answer is especially helpful in large groups where some people may not have heard it. It also gives you a moment to prepare your answer. It is unkind to humiliate people, even if they have asked a silly or irrelevant question; it is much more helpful to be positive and give them a straight answer.

Someone may have already asked a question very similar to one you've prepared; unless you have a good reason, don't ask yours as well. The key skill is looking for appropriate contributions, and needless questions will rarely count as appropriate.

**Primary school rule**
You have two ears and one mouth, so listen twice as much as you talk.

The Learning Curve

LONGMAN KEY SKILLS · COMMUNICATION · LEVEL 3

| Type of question | Purpose | Examples |
|---|---|---|
| Open | To open up discussion, to obtain an explanation or to go beyond a yes/no answer | Why do you think . . . ? How would you . . . ? What do you think about . . . ? |
| Closed | To get a short or yes/no answer | When are you going to . . . ? Is this a good or bad . . . ? |
| Follow-up | To pursue a point or to get more information | What did you mean when you said . . . ? |

# Helping others participate

## Creating a good atmosphere

**Receptive:** willing to listen to new ideas or suggestions.

One of the best ways to encourage others to participate is to create the right atmosphere for a discussion. This means making sure that people don't feel intimidated or worried about participating. Play your part in helping to make the atmosphere light and friendly, receptive and non-threatening. Give encouragement to other people's ideas, comments and suggestions.

## Sensitivity

*See also:* **Non-verbal communication**, page 15.

The key skill is trying to help you develop an awareness of others and the ability to show sensitivity when you participate in discussions. You can empathise with people by imagining what they might be thinking or feeling; try to see the discussion from their point of view. You may be able to help people feel more comfortable by using some of the techniques mentioned earlier.

**Empathy:** showing you understand how others are feeling.

How you behave and the tone of your voice can affect the ways others will react or participate. When the topic is serious, don't be flippant. Be positive, supportive and friendly, and choose an appropriate tone of voice that will help to create a good atmosphere and encourage others to feel confident and able to take part.

## Helping to include others

You are expected to show that you can help others to take part in the discussion. If someone is finding it difficult to make a contribution because they can't seem to get the group's attention, then invite them to make their point. Create an opening for them and invite them to speak. But don't turn the spotlight on someone who won't be comfortable with this attention.

**Elaborate:** to explain something you said or to give more detail on it.

You can ask follow-up questions to help someone get more involved in the group discussion. Perhaps ask them to elaborate or explain some of their comments. Ask them in a supportive way, showing that you are interested. But be sure the person actually wants to make further contributions, otherwise you may increase their anxiety. Use you empathetic skills to help you decide.

# Making a presentation

Perhaps you are dreading the moment when you have to make a presentation, but it needn't be too daunting. Let's begin with what *isn't* required of you:

- You are not expected to talk for half an hour
- You do not have to be a stand-up comedian
- Your audience need not be a large crowd

Here's what is required of you:

- Present a topic to a group of people and do it effectively
- Adapt your content and delivery to suit your audience and subject

There are three main types of presentation:

- Presentations that inform
- Presentations that persuade
- Presentations that entertain

The key skill concentrates on informing and persuading and it requires you take a complex subject as your topic.

## How long is a presentation?

The key skill does not specify a time limit for your presentation. However, it does spell out what you need to do to meet the requirements and standards expected. Concentrate on putting together a presentation that shows you have developed the necessary skills and can use appropriate techniques to get your message across.

You do not need to make your presentation long. Time is not really a major factor in the assessment requirements. You will find that by the time you have dealt with your introduction, the presentation of your topic, your conclusions, any visual aids and techniques you might use to help convey your message, you should have a presentation that is long enough.

## How large should the audience be?

Every time you see the word audience, you will probably visualise a large crowd of people; it doesn't have to be. The key skill doesn't ask that you to speak to a lot of people. The important thing is that you and your

teacher are clear about what constitutes an appropriate group size. Once you have identified a topic, you will have an idea of who might be interested in hearing a presentation on it and you will probably have an idea of what might be an appropriate size of group to speak to.

Use this part of the key skill to develop the confidence and ability to be able to present to different groups. The ability to present something is a useful skill to have. It helps develop confidence and will be valuable in many different areas. Take time to develop these skills.

# Preparing your presentation

## Give your audience a reason to listen

It's much easier to give a presentation if you've found a reason for speaking; communicate this to the audience and give them a reason for listening. Maybe identify something that needs to be presented as part of another course requirement. You could even use your presentation to revise something before an exam or an assessment. This should give your audience a reason to listen.

Another good subject for a presentation is one of your hobbies or interests. Perhaps you could speak to the school or college social club, a union meeting or a committee meeting. People who share your interest will have that as their reason to listen. Remember to focus your efforts on communicating information and developing your presenting skills. This will help you to:

- Have a clear purpose
- Identify an appropriate group
- Define your requirements

## Keep your situation in mind

Two aspects might influence your performance:

- The place where you will be speaking
- The time of day when you will speak

Investigate the layout of the room where you will be speaking; see where the audience will be seated and check how it affects your visual aids. If necessary, ask whether you can rearrange the seating or perhaps some other aspect of the room.

## How to use notes

**OHTs and OHPs**
OHTs are overhead transparencies.
OHPs are overhead projectors.
OHPs project OHTs onto a screen.

You needn't memorise the whole of your presentation and you mustn't read it like an essay. You will need to work from notes that help to jog your memory but leave you free to make eye contact, use visual aids and do all the other things that go to please an audience.

Some people like to have notes on paper, some use cards and some use paper copies of OHTs or computer screens. Experiment to see what suits you best. Here are a few general tips:

- Write or type your notes on one side only
- Use large letters that can be read at a glance
- Number each card or paper in case you drop them
- Put each main point on a separate card or paper
- Leave lots of space for last-minute changes
- Don't make too many last-minute changes
- Carry a spare set of notes

**Shrink OHTs** on a photocopier to give you wide margins for notes.

*See also:* **Using OHTs**, page 16.

Keep your notes clear; don't crowd your pages. Highlight key words or concepts to draw attention to them. Don't highlight too much or you will defeat its purpose. Maybe have a checklist of things to do before you start your presentation:

- OHP in focus
- OHTs in order
- Notes in order

# Adapting your language and delivery

## Record your method

Your method is how you adapt your presentation and the message you want to give to your audience. It includes strategies, visual aids, language and how you organise your presentation. It is everything you think will work well for the people listening to you. Make notes about your method as evidence for your portfolio. Writing about your method helps to set a context for your presentation; it explains your intentions and gives an insight into your thought processes.

## Get your tone right

Tone is your attitude towards the subject you are discussing or writing about, or your attitude towards the group you are talking to. Some tones are more appropriate than others for certain groups and purposes. An informal tone and a relaxed manner are usually effective in smaller groups and for brief presentations; a formal tone is better with larger groups and in more serious situations.

Your tone of voice is also a part of communication; for example, you may communicate anger by speaking harshly, or sympathy by speaking softly. An inappropriate voice may create negative feelings in the listener, so practise managing your tone. By speaking a little more quietly than normal, you can sometimes make people listen more attentively.

When you practise a presentation, record it on tape. Play it back to hear how you sound; your audience will probably hear something similar. Use your recording to make your presentation sound better. Perhaps you need to improve your delivery, perhaps you need to rewrite a section or perhaps you need to cut bits out.

**Alienate:** to make someone feel they are not part of what's going on, perhaps deliberately excluded.

## Vary your pitch and use pauses

The pitch of your voice is also important. Vary it to suit what you are saying and how you feel about it. Varying your pitch is an important way to keep the audience interested. Think about the way people vary their pitch when reading stories to young children. It can be quite dull to listen to a voice that hardly varies at all. Pauses add emphasis and give people time to think.

## Avoid 'gender specific' or 'culture specific' language

When you prepare and present your topic you need to be careful not to alienate people in the audience. You need to be aware that your gender (male or female) can influence the way you think and speak.

Weed out any potentially gender specific examples or aspects of your presentation (any parts that may alienate a specific group in the audience) and using more gender 'neutral' replacements. This will show that you are acknowledging the potential risk of alienating some members of your audience.

The risk of being culturally specific or showing cultural bias is a similar process. Basically, it means that you have failed to take into account the multi-cultural aspect of your audience and are using terms that may mean something to your cultural group but mean little to others. Again, the danger here is in alienating sections of your audience.

Review your work to make sure what you say can be understood by all.

## Try not to offend

There is no quicker way to alienate people than by using sexist or racist language. If you remember to include everybody, you should not have this problem. Try to use gender neutral words that include both men and women. Be careful over 'man' and similar words; use 'people' or 'humans'. Watch out for words or phrases generally considered offensive. Check your speech or writing to see how it treats these aspects and be extra careful with any jokes.

## Explain any jargon

Jargon is the specialist language found in certain jobs or subject areas. Try to avoid using jargon if you can. There will usually be someone who doesn't understand it and perhaps nobody will understand it. These are not good outcomes when your purpose is to communicate clearly. If you do wish to use important technical terms:

● Make sure the terms are crucial to your work
● Introduce them with careful explanations

> ## PUT DEFINITIONS ONTO OHTs
>
> Explain technical terms and abbreviations before you use them. One way is to write them on an OHT and leave them visible while you are speaking.

## How to get across a complex message

The key skill requires you to give a successful presentation on relatively complex topics. You can use several techniques to help your audience understand. One of the simplest is repetition. Explain the same idea more than once but each time using different words.

### Some other techniques
- Use examples that are familiar to the audience
- Ask out loud, What do I mean by this? Then answer your own question
- Use figures of speech that bring ideas to life

### Some figures of speech
- **Hyperbole:** an exaggeration to give emphasis

  **I've told you a million times.**

- **Personification:** giving human characteristics to something

  **Your presentation stood out from the crowd.**

- **Metaphor:** saying something has a quality it can't have in real life

  **Technology oils the wheels of progress by enabling new initiatives to come into being more quickly.**

- **Simile:** comparisons that use *as* or *like*

  **The month of March comes in like a lion and goes out like a lamb.**

  **My love is as tall as a mountain and as deep as the sea.**

## Using language effectively

You can make sure the type of language you use in your presentation is understood by everyone and easy to follow by keeping it simple and in the active voice. Now is not the time to show how many big words you know because your group is going to have to understand them. The point is not to show how educated you are but to show how well you can educate the audience.

Try not to use the passive voice in your presentation; using the active voice makes your presentation more dynamic and is easier for others to understand. The passive voice can make something seem dull and convoluted. Make sure that you are clear about how to recognise the passive voice and then try to avoid it in your presentation notes and speech.

Keep reminding yourself that you are going to have to say out loud what you have written. This is one way to help yourself to avoid writing long sentences or difficult words. Long sentences are difficult for the audience to follow.

# Structure and organisation

## Organising what you say

Try to draft your presentation using a computer. This will let you edit, save and spellcheck your work. It can help you change notes into OHTs. You can also create documents to record your thoughts on the audience and the techniques that you tried.

Using a computer can help you work on your presentation because it will let you save, edit and spell check your work and it can also help you turn notes into pages to be used as OHTs or computer presentations.

Remember that in preparing your presentation there are differences between what is appropriate in written English and what is appropriate or permissible when speaking. You will find that when you are presenting something, it is perfectly acceptable to:

- **Use contractions,** for example: 'are not' becomes 'aren't', 'can not' becomes 'can't'
- **Split infinitives,** for example: 'to boldly go' instead of 'to go boldly'

This relaxing of some of the formal rules of grammar allows you to use normal, everyday speech and a more conversational style that may help put your audience at ease.

When you work on the structure, think about what you want to say, when you want to say it and how you want to express it. Make your structure easy for your audience to follow. A good structure is to have a beginning, a middle and an end.

## Beginning

You need a way to introduce your subject to your listeners. Here are some questions that may be in their minds:

- Who is giving the presentation?
- What are they going to say?
- How long will it last?
- Should I take notes?

Use the introduction to set the scene for your presentation. Explain what you will be covering and give your audience a reason to be interested.

### Good things to do in your introduction
- Say how happy you are to be there (if this is appropriate).
- Connect with the audience, for example tell them how your presentation will be of help or interest to them, or why it is important.

- Start with a catchy title that you can expand on. Think of how newspapers use headlines to attract attention and stimulate interest in an article.
- Ask a question in the introduction that you can go on to answer it in the main part of your presentation. Then use your final answer to give you a strong conclusion at the end.

### Bad things to do in your introduction
- Start trying to organise you notes, OHTs or equipment (you should have done this already).
- Admit you're not prepared.
- Admit you're nervous.
- Try to be too clever and start with a joke.
- Get a person's name wrong.
- Use clichés.

## The middle

Generally speaking, this is where the group you talk to is at most risk of switching-off. If you are going to list and talk about different things, tell the audience clearly what point you are referring to and when you are making the final point. Most importantly try not to have a long list. Aim for no more than three or four points in the list, otherwise people's attention will fade.

This is the part of the presentation where you need to put the techniques you have learned to good effect and try to keep the group's interest. If your presentation is informative, this is where the information is to be communicated. If your presentation is trying to persuade people, this is where you locate your main argument.

There are a number of ways to organise your presentation; here are a few examples:

- **Using a list**: It doesn't matter if it's A, B, C or 1, 2, 3; this way of organising your presentation is clear, simple and easy for the group to follow. However, if some points are more important than others be careful to let people know.
- **'Problem–solution'/'cause and effect'**: With this method, you start by describing a problem, explaining the different issues that might be involved then end with a possible solution. This is well suited to presentations about designing or working to a brief (the problem) or meeting a challenge. In the cause and effect method you describe what happened, go over the reasons and then explain the results.

### Holding it all together
However you choose to organise your presentation, you need to spend time making sure that the different parts all fit together and that your points are in a logical sequence. The sequence may be determined by the fact that some points are more important than others or that some points are of more interest to the group.

## The end

Get to the end on time! The next best thing you can do is let the audience know that you are coming to an end. Use words and phrases that the group will recognise as meaning you are nearing the finish and making your concluding points. Recap main points briefly and bring your presentation to a strong conclusion (a definite ending).

Make sure you keep the conclusion brief and to the point. Don't tell people you are coming to an end then keep rambling on. You might even boil down your message to one key point, for example: 'If there is one thing you need to take away from this talk, it is this. . .'.

Don't introduce something new, even if it is something that you forgot to say. This is a sign that you were not properly organised. There might be an opportunity to mention it if there are going to be questions afterwards. Remember, you are trying to make the conclusion 'round off' what you have said, making your presentation look complete. A good start and a good finish can make all the difference.

## In a nutshell

Repetition can be a fault when you write reports or essays however is presentations it can be helpful for those listening. If you plan to use notes, make them clear and brief. Refer to your notes, but do not read straight from them. You should be reminded of what you want to say just by glancing at a key word or heading in your notes. Make your speech as accessible as possible to your audience. Keep your language clear and conversational, keep your sentences short, keep a steady pace, make sure your points are in a logical sequence and that there is a clear transition between them.

## Keeping the audience interested

### Find out about the group

You need to spend time thinking about your potential audience. Knowledge about your group, if used effectively, can help your presentation go well. Key factors to consider are:

- **Size of the group:** This is important in helping you determine which visual aids to use, how many handouts to prepare, or whether you can be more or less formal.
- **What the group thinks or knows about your topic:** This will help you get an idea of whether they know the basics of your topic, will understand some of the jargon (technical language) or are even likely to be interested in your topic. Showing how you are going to attempt to deal with any of these issues will generate evidence for your key skill portfolio.
- **Adapting your talk so that it relates to your group:** You can do this by 'localising' references in your presentation to help the audience understand. It could be examples adapted to explain what might happen in the group's local area or local environment.

# Non-verbal communication

Non-verbal communication describes your eye contact, body movements, gestures and your overall appearance during your presentation. All these aspects can send messages to your audience and create impressions of what you are like. Some impressions will improve the impact of your presentation and these are the ones you should try to create.

## Facial expressions

Your face can reveal a lot about your thoughts and feelings; use it to animate your presentation and bring your words to life:

- Smiling creates a friendly atmosphere, it shows joy and pleasure
- Frowning shows puzzlement, disapproval and concern
- Raised eyebrows indicate surprise

## Gestures and body movements

You can use gestures to point things out or to add emphasis, perhaps by shaking your fist. Appropriate gestures will complement your words and make your presentation more interesting and enjoyable. The skill is in choosing them appropriately. Too many gestures, inappropriate gestures or poorly timed gestures may make your audience lose interest or detract attention from your message.

## Using your hands

You can also use your hands to add emphasis and enliven your presentation, but don't let them become a distraction. See how other speakers use their hands and decide which of their movements were effective. Always be aware of what your hands are doing. Once you have finished a hand movement, return your hands to a neutral position, perhaps in your lap or by your side. This prevents you from using your hands unwittingly and sending messages you may not want to. Try to avoid:

- **Hands in pockets:** you cannot use them to gesture.
- **Rattling change:** this distracts people.
- **Fiddling:** this indicates stress or nervousness; items that people often fiddle with are jewellery, clothing and spectacles.

## Standing comfortably

There is a lot of talk about the best way to stand, but normally you should have a straight back, your feet apart (about a shoulder's width) and your arms free to move. But above all, be comfortable and have your hands free. Avoid leaning or slouching; don't sway about.

## Making eye contact

Practise making eye contact. Try to involve your listeners in what you are saying. Move your gaze around; do not rest on the same few people all the time. By making eye contact with your listeners, you will help them to feel directly involved. Avoid staring into the distance or looking over the heads of your listeners. Maintain eye contact for about a sentence before moving your gaze to somebody else; try not to flit rapidly from person to person. Eye contact helps to keep your listeners alert. It takes practice to develop but is probably the most effective aspect of body language. If you are shy of using it in your presentations, do persevere for the results are well worth the effort.

# Using visual aids

Visual aids, such as OHTs and flip charts, can raise your confidence. They help you to pace your presentation and remind you what you want to say. They give the audience something else to look at. The most common visual aids are overhead transparencies (OHTs), flip charts and computer presentations,

## Using OHTs

Some computer packages may have templates to help you with OHTs.

Visual aids can be a useful means of increasing your confidence. They can help you:

- Pace yourself better
- Keep you on track
- Help you remember what you want to say.

They also give the audience something other than you to focus on.

### *Using overhead transparencies (OHTs)*

Overhead transparencies (OHTs) can be useful because they can guide others through your presentation and making you less reliant on checking your notes. If you choose to use OHTs try to create them using a computer. Some computer packages may have templates to help you.

When you are happy with the look of the pages (for example: checked that the typeface is large enough, the pages are not too full of text and are broken down into correct headings to assist the flow of the presentation) print them out. Then you can photocopy the pages onto the OHTs. If you are going to use OHTs, spend some time making them look neat and professional. Use the computer to put a border around the transparency, and use a 'header' or 'footer' to number and label the pages. Numbering them will help prevent confusion if you drop them and have to put them back in order.

## HINTS FOR USING OHTS

Here are some simple rules to remember when using OHTs:
- Don't put too much information on each OHT
- Don't let them totally dominate your presentation
- Try and keep to the same font
- Don't get carried away using bold or italics

### *Only put the important information on the OHT*

Over-reliance on OHTs will make it difficult for you to use eye contact to engage the audience because either you or they will be looking at the OHTs. The presence of an OHP can also restrict your movement and your ability to use non-verbal communication. However, you can use the OHP to control the speed of the presentation and the focus of the audience by only partially showing some of the text at first and revealing more as you work through it. Covering your OHT with a blank sheet of paper and moving it down slowly to reveal more text or information does this. This means you are controlling the rate you want your audience to see the information. This is particularly useful if you have a list and you want to discuss each point one at a time.

OHTs are a good way to focus the audience attention, though they tend not to work as well with larger groups. But beware, they are there to help you present, they should never be the presentation. OHT techniques need to be practised and it will take you some time to develop the confidence to use them.

Consider making copies of your 'overheads' to give out at the end of your presentation but make sure that you tell your audience at the outset that you are going to do this or they will waste time and attention taking notes unnecessarily. Having copies of your OHTs available with you is also handy as a precaution if the bulb on the OHP fails.

If you have a series of headings, ideas or concepts on the OHTs then consider giving copies out at the start and this will help provide a structure for people taking notes.

## BEFORE YOUR PRESENTATION

- Check that the OHP is ready, in working order and, in case of technical failure, have a back-up plan.
- Put one of your OHTs on the projector and check that the machine is correctly focused.
- Use a pointer and always point at the OHT on the machine not the projected image on the screen.
- Know where the OHP cable is and keep away from it.

## Charts, diagrams and graphs

Charts, graphs and diagrams are great for numerical information or statistics. They can be used on OHTs or flip charts. You can also use tables as long as they are not too big. Tables with many entries may be okay to read in books and journals, even on computer screens, but they rarely work well as part of a presentation. Only use statistics when they make your points clearer; don't use them to hide any gaps in your argument or weaknesses in your preparation. Here are some tips:

- Keep your graphs and diagrams simple and clear
- Give them a title and label the important features
- Choose appropriate scales to illustrate your points
- Use them sparingly; don't overwhelm your audience

## Flip charts

Often best with small groups, flip charts work well when your presentation covers clearly defined stages. Put each stage on a separate sheet, then as the presentation moves from stage to stage, you can flip your chart from sheet to sheet. Each time you flip, give the chart a tilt to draw people's attention. Some speakers put full details on the flip chart before they begin the presentation; other speakers set up the headings and write in more information as they go along. You can follow most of the rules for OHTs and here are some that are specific to flip charts:

- Write clearly in letters big enough to read
- Do not put too many words on each sheet
- Use pens that have dark colours, e.g. black
- Don't talk to the chart, talk to the audience
- Give people time to read what you have written
- Put the pen down after writing; don't fiddle

## Handouts

Handouts save a lot of note taking for the audience and may help you to guide people through your material. But, almost certainly, some people will prefer to read the handouts instead of listening to you. One way around this is to distribute them at the end. Always tell the audience at the beginning if this is what you are going to do. Long handouts or detailed material could be distributed at the start or finish of your presentation.

## Presenting work using computers

Computers can help you to show your work to other people, such as presenting the results of a project. The word processor, spreadsheet and graphics programs described earlier give you plenty of choices for making your work look good.

Whichever method you use to present your work, it is important to make a good impression. Here are some things you can do to check and improve your work:

- Check that the content is relevant – don't use it just because you have it.
- Select the important information and make sure it stands out.
- Put lots of space between items.
- Beware of using too many fancy effects.
- Use a spellchecker then use a human being.
- Ask other people what they think.

### Presentation programs

Specialised programs, e.g. PowerPoint, are designed to help you make materials for presentations and then to run the presentations. You can use presentation programs for the following purposes:

- Create OHTs or slides
- Store OHTs and slides
- Run a slide show from a computer
- Fade in and out between slides
- Print paper copies of all slides
- Print summaries of slides

**Some presentations**
covers for projects
text for projects
project results
announcements
financial information
marketing information
automatic slide shows

*Typical presentation slide combining text and graphics*

Most presentation programs work in the same general way and have the following basic features:

- **Design options** allow you to choose different styles of ready-made slide plus ways of laying out information and graphics.
- **Notes** provide information to go with the slides.
- **Clip art** can be added along with other pictures.
- **Graphs and charts** can be imported from other packages.
- **Edit commands** allow work to be changed using undo, cut, paste and copy.
- **View** generates different types of slide, summaries, speaker notes and handout notes.
- **Slide show** allows you to show the slides full-size on the computer screen or on a projector screen; there is the option to add timing and let the slide show run automatically.
- **Slide effects** include special effects as slides change and added sound effects.

---

## FORMAL DOCUMENTS: KEEP THEM SIMPLE

As the purpose of a document or a presentation becomes more formal, simple styles and effects become more appropriate.

---

Presentation software can help you to create a striking visual presentation, with 'wizards' to help you get started and a spell-checker to save your blushes. People like to have good quality handouts and using a package like PowerPoint to give your handouts a professional look will impress. However, information technology (IT) software can't write or deliver your presentation for you so think of it as the icing on the cake. You will have to create the good material first, then work with IT to find effective ways to communicate the message.

Keep in mind your purpose, which is to communicate information and not to put on a light show. Don't detract from the message of the presentation with too fancy a delivery. IT can help you with your style but don't forget your substance.

## Film or video

A film clip or a short video can often convey information more effectively than several pages of text. You can easily pause a video to:

- Ask a question
- Discuss a point
- Examine an image
- Replay an action
- Make a few notes

Video allows many people to follow your information together and all at the same pace. You can fast forward to skip bits out and you can use the counter to find the bits you want. Videos provide a starting point for discussion, and they're great for teaching, briefing and presenting. When it comes to audiences, it's often better to stimulate their eyes than their ears. Here are some other uses for video:

- Analysing your own performance
- Recording a project over time
- Creating some moving-image art

# Reading and synthesising information

There are many reasons why we read:

- To obtain information
- To learn how to do something
- To check a text is accurate
- For recreation and pleasure

**Synthesise:** combine several items into a coherent whole.

The most important thing is to understand what you are reading. It is not enough just to understand the words themselves, you need to comprehend what they mean. Short passages are usually quite easy to comprehend but longer works require greater concentration, especially if you have to remember several ideas at once. Take notes as you go along; they will help to jog your memory.

## Finding and using sources

### Selecting appropriate material

A lot of your information will probably come from text, but some may come from emails, telephone conversations or face-to-face discussions. Here are the main text-based sources:

- Textbooks and reference books
- Directories and dictionaries
- Letters, memos and emails
- Newspapers and magazines
- Teletext pages, e.g. Ceefax
- Websites on the Internet
- CD-ROM encyclopedias, etc.
- Exhibition guides and catalogues
- Library collections and museums
- Posters, leaflets and other publicity
- Manufacturers' catalogues and data
- Government and commercial reports
- Research papers, theses and essays

Be clear about why you are gathering information. Maybe you wish to find out about a particular writer. Where do you start? You could ask other people to give you some suggestions. They may give you a book list or suggest somewhere to visit.

## Libraries

A library contains a large number of information sources. To help you find what you want, it is organised into different subject areas. Small libraries may use a small number of broad categories; big libraries may use a large number of narrow categories. You can identify the material you want by looking at the library's catalogue. Some libraries still keep their catalogue on small index cards held in drawers and arranged in alphabetical order. However, most now store this information electronically for access by computer.

### Basic details for books and periodicals

- Title of book, journal, newspaper or magazine
- Name of author, editor, contributor or columnist
- Publication date, volume number and pages
- Name of publisher

# Using the Internet

The Internet is a system which allows many computers in the world to join together a system of link-ups. The Internet is effectively a huge database of information and the rules for retrieving data are similar to those used to query databases. At home we usually link to the Internet via our phone line but larger computers in the Internet are connected by high-speed telecommunication links which use cable and satellite.

## The Web

The Internet can be used in different ways but the two main uses for most people are **email**, described in a later section, and the **Web**. The Web is part of the Internet where organisations or people have pages of text and pictures. From these pages you can find information, buy goods or jump to other pages. You get directly to a **website** by entering the address into your browser. Website addresses often look like this:

www.name.com

www.name.co.uk

## Looking up websites

To use the Internet you subscribe to an **internet service provider** (ISP) who has a computer which links you to the Web. Your local computer is connected to your ISP by using a modem which sends digital signals along the phone

**Some ISPs**
AOL
BT Internet
Bun
Claranet
Compuserve
Freeserve
Virgin Net

connections. Your computer will have an icon for dial-up connections. Click on this icon to connect to the Internet; you may need to enter a password before the modem begins to dial. The computers at work, in an Internet cafe, or in a college are usually permanently connected to the Internet.

When you're online to the Web you will use a **browser**, such as **Microsoft Explorer** or **Netscape Navigator**. The browser is a computer program which displays webpages.

## Using a browser

All types of browser work in a similar manner and have a banner along the top of the screen where you click to give commands. The main commands are described in the following table.

| Icon | Effect when clicked |
| --- | --- |
| Address or Go to | Allows you to enter the address or name of a website that you want |
| Back | Takes you back to the webpage you just visited |
| Forward | Moves you forward to a webpage you just came from |
| Stop | Stops loading the current page |
| Refresh or Reload | Loads a new version of the current page; useful when a page is incomplete or often updated |
| Home | Goes to the page seen when your browser opens; this can be changed to whatever you want |
| Search | Begins options which search by keyword |
| Favourites or Bookmarks | Drops down a list of favourite websites you have marked in the past |
| Mail | Connects to email |
| History | Gives a list of the websites you have visited in past days or weeks |
| Mail | Opens the options for using email |
| Print | Prints out the webpage shown on-screen |

### STOP BUTTON

Click the **Stop** button if a connection is very slow; you can try again at a less busy time.

**Web addresses**
Most website addresses start with **www**.

The most important thing is to get started using the blank line near the top of the screen called **Address** or **Go to**. Suppose you want to see the website with address www.bbc.co.uk:

● Type it into the address box of your browser.
● Check you have typed it correctly.
● Press the **Enter** key.
● Wait for the webpage to download into your computer.

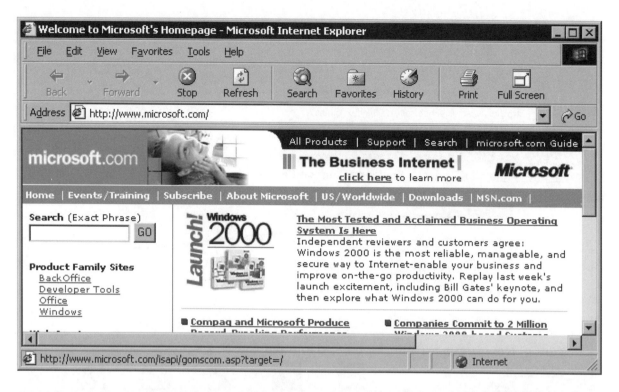

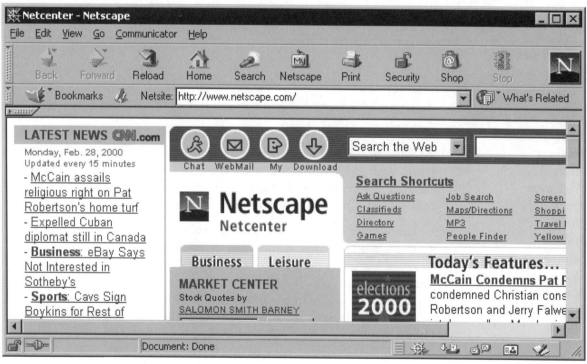

*Internet browsers: Internet Explorer and Netscape*

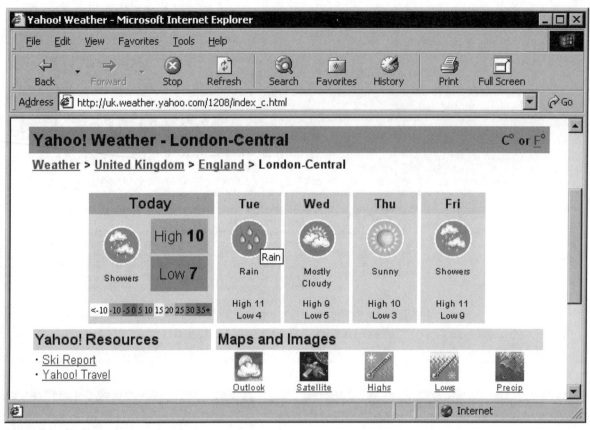

*Typical Web page*

## Popular search engines

AltaVista
AskJeeves
Excite
Google
HotBot
Infoseek
Lycos
MSN Search
Northern Light
Yahoo

## Searching the Internet

The Internet joins you to the information held by thousands of computers world wide, so it is the largest database in the world. Somewhere on the Internet are websites with answers to your questions, but they have to be found. You can reach this information in the following two ways:

- **Go directly** because you know the website address.
- **Use a search engine** to trawl the net for relevant websites.

### Search engines

Some well-known search engines are described in the following table. Some of the engines let you enter your question in general language. Others work better if you use the tricks for advanced searches.

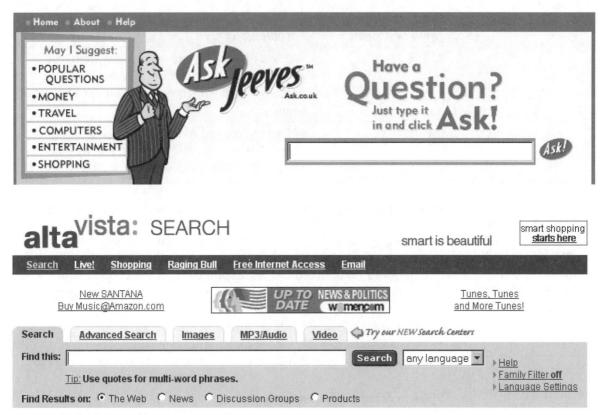

*Two typical search engines (AskJeeves and AltaVista)*

| Search engine and address | Notes |
|---|---|
| AskJeeves<br>**www.ask.co.uk** | Good site for beginners. Allows you to ask questions in plain English such as, Where is information about xyz? Some of the answers may be too general |
| MSN Search<br>**www.search.msn.com** | Good site for beginners and good links to other information |
| Yahoo<br>**www.yahoo.co.uk** | Can be browsed by categories or can be searched by keyword |
| AltaVista<br>**www.altavista.com** | Indexes more webpages than many engines. Also has advanced search option to focus your search |

## Advanced searches

Some types of search involve the logic of combinations. This is particularly true when searching huge databases like the Internet. For example using AND: this will force the search engine to look for references where the words are joined together. Here is how you search for websites on blue whales.

| Extra search conditions (word or symbol) | Possible effect |
| --- | --- |
| AND<br>+ | Will find references which include the word *blue* joined with the word *whales*. This condition will probably find the references to the particular type of whale |
| OR<br>– | Will find references which include either the word *blue* or the word *whales*. This condition will find thousands of references you don't want |

## Skimming and scanning

**Skimming:** looking through text to get a general idea of its content.
**Scanning:** looking at text and images to identify relevant information.

Skimming and scanning are two techniques that help you find the information you need quickly without having to read the whole text. They can also help you find time to use more sources of information in your search. This saves you time and allows you to focus your concentration only on what you need to read.

Once you have identified the author or subject areas you are interested in you can begin to look for the information you need. The more specific your search, the easier it will be to skim text for the relevant headings.

### Skim to locate information quickly

Skimming can help you get a quick, general idea of the content of a book, magazine or report and will give you important clues about where the information you need might be found. The contents page and index are useful starting points, helping you locate likely pages that may contain the information you want. Scanning these pages will help you determine whether or not the information you need is there.

Generally speaking, skimming will help you get an impression of a text and help you find out about it. It doesn't help you establish what is in the

### Scan to understand text quickly

Scanning can help you focus your search more. You do this by quickly looking over the text, following up any clues given to you in the index or contents page, to look for the exact information you need. Scanning text will help you zoom in on the information you need.

Scanning is a focused and shorthand form of reading. It involves:

- Picking out key words in the text
- Using key words as landmarks in the text so that you stay focused
- Saving time by not reading every word on the page in the hope of finding what you want

Scanning helps you spot the key words that are relevant to what you want to find out, so that you can then concentrate on reading the appropriate sections.

In addition to scanning text, you can also scan visual material for information for example a static two-dimensional (2D) image like a photograph or moving 2D images like a film. The process of scanning this type of material is the same as scanning text except that your 'landmarks' are images rather than words. Other 2D images that you can scan include:

- Graphs, charts, tables
- Diagrams, maps, plans
- Drawings and paintings

You may even be scanning three dimensional (3D) forms like:

- Sculpture
- Buildings
- Equipment
- Landscapes

Reading texts, numbers and images can provide you with information that will help all aspects of your learning. You must make sure that you collect and record information that is relevant and in a form that will be useful to you later. Once you have located the information you need you should read it carefully making sure you understand what is being said. Skimming and scanning are not substitutes for reading properly, they are just techniques to help you find what you need to begin reading quickly.

When you come to make notes on something you will need to have read it properly making sure you either thoroughly understand what is written down or know what you need to get help in order to understand it. When you start reading a text properly you may have to go back to the beginning or a chapter of section in order to get a better idea of what the information is about. Once you have a clear understanding of the something you can start recording it.

## Recording

Once you have found some relevant information, make a note of where it's located. There are three good reasons for this:

- It will be easier to find in the future
- You may need to compile a bibliography
- You can compare notes with other people

### Making notes

Making notes is an important part of collecting information. Your notes provide a useful record of the information you have read and will help you to understand the text. When you come to write a report or essay based on your notes they will help you plan your work, be useful in helping you decide what to write and will also jog your memory. The ability to take clear notes will also help you revise for tests or exams.

You need to think carefully about the information you record as notes. When taking notes you need to ask yourself. 'Do I need this information?' and 'How and where will I use it?' Good notes are not simply passages of text copied out again in your own handwriting – you should try to use

your own words. This will help show you understand what you are taking notes about and will mean that you are more likely to understand the notes when you read them later.

Leave spaces between notes and always have a margin. This gives you the opportunity to go back afterwards and add to them.

## HINTS ON RECORDING INFORMATION

- Organise your notes around key themes written as headings
- Make notes on each text you read, with the author and title stated at the top and where appropriate the chapter or page numbers your notes come from.
- Note down real names exactly
- Always write down any quotations you intend to use exactly as they appear in the text your are reading
- Record exactly where the quote comes from because you will need to show this when you use it.

Once you have collected the information you need and recorded your findings you will be ready to summarise your material.

You need to establish a way of taking notes that suits you. The most important thing to keep in mind is that you will need to use you notes either for revision or for an essay or report you need to produce so make sure they are clear.

# Writing documents

Written communication is valued because it provides a permanent record and can be made available to many people at a time. Written instructions are often better than verbal instructions because there is a record that they were issued. It is much easier to dispute a verbal instruction. The person who has to carry out the instruction can refer to your document and they don't have to rely on their memory. A well-written instruction has a good chance of being carried out successfully but it could still be misinterpreted; a verbal instruction runs a greater risk of misinterpretation.

## Types of document

### Formal letter

#### *Letter formats*
Formal letters are used in business-to-business communication. They are also sent by governments, schools, charities and other organisations. Often they follow a house style which dictates their format on the page and perhaps a few sentences at the start and the finish. Of the three main formats, illustrated on the next page, fully blocked is the most common:

- Indented
- Semi-blocked
- Fully blocked (there is an example of a fully blocked letter on page 34)

#### *Letter content and tone*
The tone of a letter influences how the recipient will respond. It's as important as the format, so choose it carefully to suit your purpose:

- Confirming arrangements
- Querying details
- Updating figures
- Reporting progress
- Listing results
- Proposing ideas
- Trying to persuade

A positive tone is generally more effective than a negative tone. Focus on what you can do, not what you can't. Try to be constructive rather than defensive. If you have to write to someone about mistakes they have made,

**Tones of voice**
cooperative
motivating
persuasive
promotional
factual

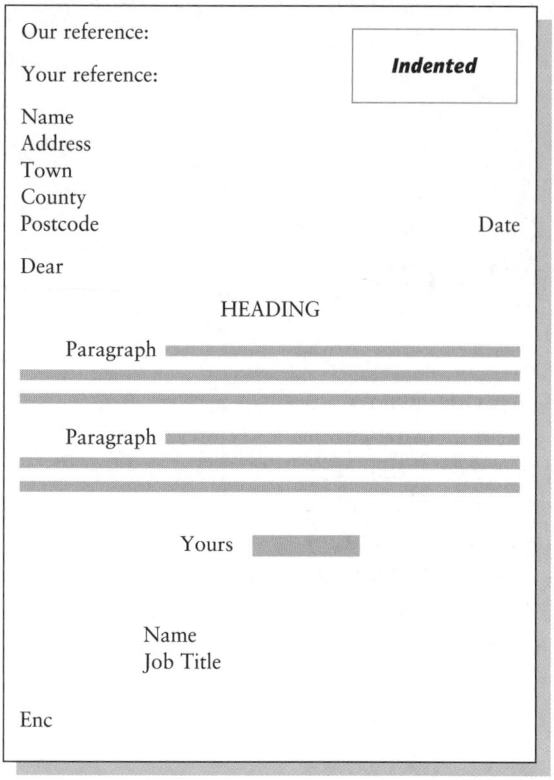

**Indented**

Our reference:

Your reference:

Name
Address
Town
County
Postcode                                    Date

Dear

HEADING

    Paragraph ▬▬▬▬▬▬▬▬▬▬▬▬▬▬▬▬
▬▬▬▬▬▬▬▬▬▬▬▬▬▬▬▬▬▬▬▬
▬▬▬▬▬▬▬▬▬▬▬▬▬▬▬▬▬▬▬▬

    Paragraph ▬▬▬▬▬▬▬▬▬▬▬▬▬▬▬▬
▬▬▬▬▬▬▬▬▬▬▬▬▬▬▬▬▬▬▬▬
▬▬▬▬▬▬▬▬▬▬▬▬▬▬▬▬▬▬▬▬

      Yours ▬▬▬▬

     Name
     Job Title

Enc

---

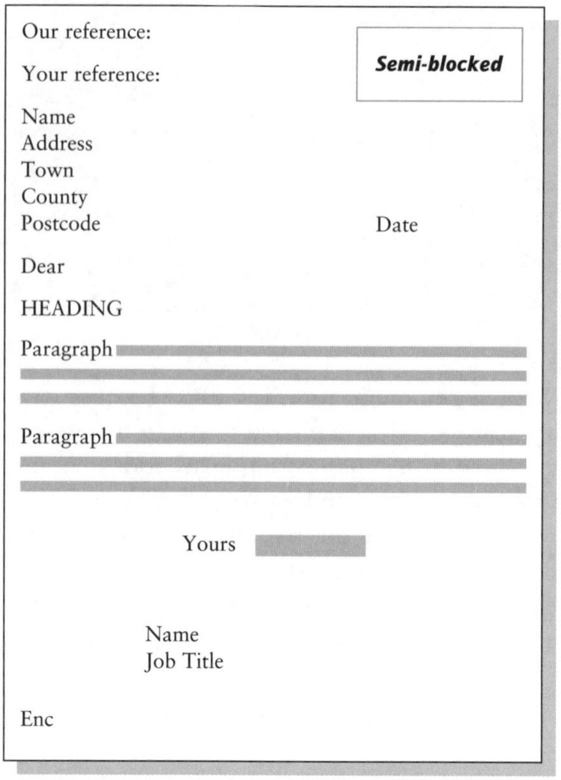

**Semi-blocked**

Our reference:

Your reference:

Name
Address
Town
County
Postcode                                    Date

Dear

HEADING

Paragraph ▬▬▬▬▬▬▬▬▬▬▬▬▬▬▬▬
▬▬▬▬▬▬▬▬▬▬▬▬▬▬▬▬▬▬▬▬
▬▬▬▬▬▬▬▬▬▬▬▬▬▬▬▬▬▬▬▬

Paragraph ▬▬▬▬▬▬▬▬▬▬▬▬▬▬▬▬
▬▬▬▬▬▬▬▬▬▬▬▬▬▬▬▬▬▬▬▬

      Yours ▬▬▬▬

     Name
     Job Title

Enc

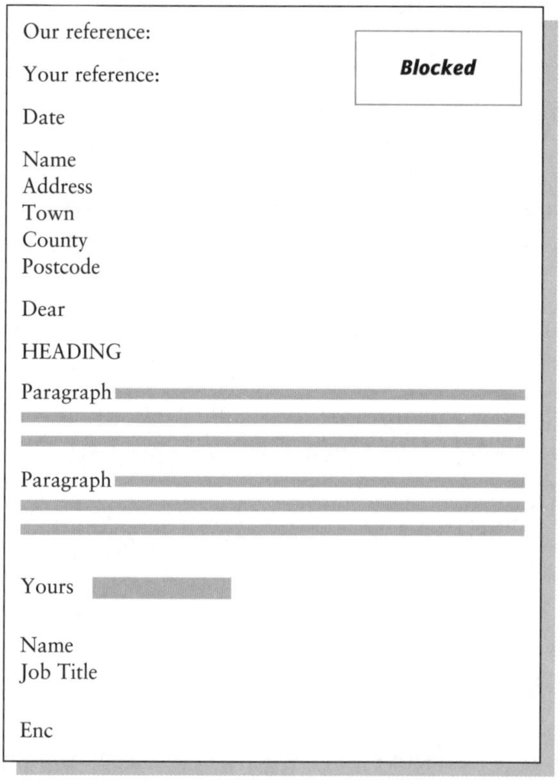

---

**Blocked**

Our reference:

Your reference:

Date

Name
Address
Town
County
Postcode

Dear

HEADING

Paragraph ▬▬▬▬▬▬▬▬▬▬▬▬▬▬▬▬
▬▬▬▬▬▬▬▬▬▬▬▬▬▬▬▬▬▬▬▬

Paragraph ▬▬▬▬▬▬▬▬▬▬▬▬▬▬▬▬
▬▬▬▬▬▬▬▬▬▬▬▬▬▬▬▬▬▬▬▬

Yours ▬▬▬▬

Name
Job Title

Enc

it may not be wise to adopt an admonishing tone, even if you're quite angry. Take some time to deal with your feelings then write a constructive letter that benefits both of you. The letter on page 28 has a tone that is both critical and cooperative.

### Letters as evidence

You can submit a formal letter as part of your key skill evidence. Either write a reply to a letter you have received or write to someone and invite them to write back. Here are some possible subjects for a letter:

- A planned activity or event
- A technical enquiry or issue
- Ideas or views
- A technical report
- Some statistical data

Use the flow chart and remember that all letters have a purpose. Here are three ways to make your purpose clear:

- Include all the relevant information
- Use short sentences and simple words
- Fit your letter into one side of A4 paper

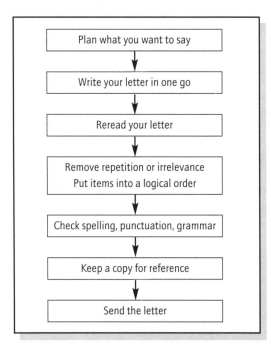

Plan what you want to say

↓

Write your letter in one go

↓

Reread your letter

↓

Remove repetition or irrelevance
Put items into a logical order

↓

Check spelling, punctuation, grammar

↓

Keep a copy for reference

↓

Send the letter

## Memos

Memorandums, or memos, are sent between people within an organisation. They are rarely sent to people outside; letters are used for that. Memos should be short and straight to the point. Their purpose is to give information or to jog someone's memory, and their format is designed to save time and space for both writer and reader. Memos are often delivered on paper but many are now sent by email.

**Learning for Life Academy**
**College Square, Camford, Camfordshire, CR2 1SX**
**Tel 01227 614758 Fax 01227 614759**

Our reference: AP/JU/45IPros98

Your reference: TB63

*Example of a fully blocked letter*

3April 1998

Mr T Jones
36 New Town Close
Camford
Camfordshire
CR4 1ST

Dear Mr Jones

**Entry for 1998/99 Prospectus**

Further to my letter of 16 March, I write to remind you that the copy deadline for our next prospectus has now passed and I am concerned that I do not appear to have received your entry. This is now critical because without it the academy will not be able to advertise your course.

I regret that it is not possible to extend the copy deadline further; it is imperative that material be submitted to the printer to enable her to produce the prospectus in time for our publicity mailing next month.

It may be that you are experiencing some difficulty that has prevented you from meeting the deadline. If so, please let me know if there is any way in which I can be of assistance.

Indeed, it is possible that this letter has crossed with yours to me containing your entry, in which case all will be well. If not, would you kindly send yours to me by return of post? I enclose a prepaid envelope for your convenience.

I look forward to hearing from you.

Yours sincerely

A Perkins (Ms)
**Director, Learning for Life Academy**

Enc:  prepaid envelope

## Agendas and minutes

An agenda is a formal notice that a meeting will take place. Normally sent out five or ten days before the meeting, it tells you when and where the meeting will happen plus the items up for discussion. At the meeting someone usually takes notes on the main items of business. These notes are written up as the minutes, given out at the next meeting and approved by the people who attend. Sometimes items do need correction and these corrections appear in the next set of minutes. One person is usually elected to take minutes for all the meetings in a year; they are known as the minutes secretary or perhaps the committee secretary. Minutes are a written record of:

- Any agreements reached
- Any decisions made
- Any actions to be taken

**LEARNING FOR LIFE ACADEMY**

Programme Planning Committee

Friday 14 January 2000 (2pm)

Room 1
Senate Building, College Square, Camford

Ann Hack
Committee Secretary

### AGENDA

> *Example of agenda format*

1. APOLOGIES FOR ABSENCE

2. MINUTES OF THE LAST MEETING

    The minutes of the meeting held on 23 December 1999 are attached, for confirmation

3. MATTERS ARISING

4. PROPOSALS FOR NEW PROGRAMMES

    i.   Campus provision – Paper LLA/003
    ii.  Off-campus provision – Paper LLA/004

5. LEARNING AIDS FOR NEW COURSES

    Dr Jones to report.

6. LIBRARY EXTENSION

    Ms M Forbes, estates and buildings officer, to report,

7. ANY OTHER BUSINESS

8. DATE OF NEXT MEETING

## Notes of discussions

People meet in groups to have all kinds of discussions, formal and informal. Sometimes you may need to record what happened, so note taking is a useful skill. If the notes are for your own use, they can be in any format you like but maybe choose something you will understand when you come to reread them.

## Written reports

A report is a useful way of presenting information and results. Here are some examples:

- A review of a product, performance or idea
- A progress record on a plan or proposal
- An outcome of an enquiry or investigation

**Report:** key points written up in a clear and quickly readable form.

*LEARNING FOR LIFE ACADEMY*
MINUTES OF THE PROGRAMME PLANNING COMMITTEE
**14 January 2000**

Present:    Ms J Deane (in the chair)
            Mr P Fox
            Ms A Hack (committee secretary)
            Mr L Hunt
            Mr C Johnson
            Ms P Mack

*Example of*

*minutes format*

In attendance: Ms M Forbes

**17  APOLOGIES FOR ABSENCE**
Apologies for absence were received from Dr Perks and Mr Wiggins.

**18  MINUTES OF THE LAST MEETING**
The minutes of the meeting held on 23 December 1999, previously circulated, were confirmed.

**19  MATTERS ARISING**
**13  Entries for the 2000/2001 Prospectus**
It was agreed that the deadline be extended to 30 April 2000.
**15  Publicity Working Party Report - Autumn 1999**
A report was laid upon the table. Mr Hunt apologised for the delay in its production. Members approved the report.

**20  PROPOSALS FOR NEW PROGRAMMES**
**20.1  Campus provision**
Six new proposals had been received. Ms Mack pointed out that the reduced number of teaching rooms in H-block meant that only six courses would be accommodated there in 2000/2001 instead of the usual twelve.
**20.2  Off-campus provision**
As a result of the reduction in the size of the campus provision, the number of programmes held off-campus would be increased. Ms Mack invited committee members to submit proposals to her office by the end of March.

**21  LEARNING AIDS FOR NEW COURSES**
Dr Jones reported that the library had allocated an additional £3000 to the academy's budget for new purchases and advised that a proportion of this could be used for audioTvisual aids (tapes and videos).

**22  LIBRARY EXTENSION**
Ms Forbes attended for this item. She advised that the site for the new extension had been surveyed and preliminary plans were being prepared. The committee advised Ms Forbes of the urgency of this matter.

**23**  There being no further business, the meeting closed at 3.45 pm.

**24  DATE OF NEXT MEETING**
It was agreed that the next meeting would be held on 31 January 2000 at 2pm.

- An account of an event, incident or happening
- A bulletin to highlight a technical problem
- A summary of a telephone conversation
- A digest of several other documents

Reports usually have this structure:

- **Introduction:** state your aims and purposes.
- **Middle:** present your findings.
- **Conclusion:** analyse and evaluate your findings.
- **Recommendations:** suggest what to do about your findings.

Some reports have extra sections:

- **For action:** concrete measures that come after recommendations.
- **Appendices:** important data, calculations, etc., tidied to the end.

The items in the appendices may be very important but they are often long or complicated and do not fit easily into the main body of the report. Putting them near the end makes them easy to refer to and stops the report's text becoming horribly broken up.

A more formal report may begin with its terms of reference – the people it's written for and the topics it's allowed to investigate – then a statement of its procedures – how it's allowed to gather information. Most reports are signed and dated at the end.

Use numbered headings to guide readers through your report. Write a first draft then amend it, perhaps several times, to arrive at your final version. It should be easy to read and simple to understand. Before you submit your report, forget the words for a moment and see how it looks overall:

- Is your design good? Does it make an impact?
- Is it the right length? Not too much or too little?

## BEFORE YOU WRITE A REPORT

- Check all the requirements, e.g.
  - word count
  - page layout
  - typefaces
- Check who you're writing for so you get the tone and style right

Prepare your first draft by jotting down the main headings followed by some brief notes. Indicate where you want illustrations, graphs or tables. When you come to write it:

- Keep an eye on the word count; don't write too much
- Assemble your ideas logically; don't jump about
- Avoid pointless repetition; don't repeat yourself

## Project write-ups

The main difference between a project write-up and an extended essay is that a project write-up is likely to use more graphs and tables, more diagrams and illustrations. Have a look at the previous section, on reports, and the next section, on essays, and use the advice there to suit the kind of write-up you're aiming for.

## Essays

The essay form gives you an opportunity to use a range of writing styles. Listen to your tone of voice; you'll hear when it sounds right. The trick is to put the right words in the right places. If a sentence doesn't sound right, you can do two things:

- Keep the words the same but rearrange their order
- Keep the order the same but change one or two words

Here are some other guidelines:

- Hold the reader's interest
- Adopt a logical structure
- Always keep to the point
- Use clear, simple language
- Write short sentences
- Choose an appropriate tone
- Collect enough evidence
- Reference all your sources
- Quote people accurately
- Avoid personal prejudices
- Be sparing with anecdotes

---

**EVERY ESSAY SHOULD HAVE**

- An introduction to say what it's about
- An exposition to cover its main points
- A conclusion to wind it up nicely

---

## Referencing sources of information

Extended documents like essays or reports may contains quotes from other documents or publications, and you must include correct attributions that include details of the original author or source of the information. This shows readers where the ideas came from, as well as indicates the range of sources you used to produce your work. Using information from other sources can help increase the credibility of your work.

There are two main ways of giving information about your sources. The first is through a bibliography. A bibliography is an alphabetical list of all the sources you use to produce your work. For each source document or publication the bibliography lists:

- Author's surname and initials
- Year of publication
- Title
- Place of publication and name of publisher
- Page numbers (if relevant)

Example of a reference in a bibliography:

Thoreau, H.D. (1993) *Walden and other writings*. New York: Barnes and Noble, p. 7

References to magazine and newspaper articles should include the title of the article title and of the publication, and the publication date. Your bibliography should also list any electronic sources of information such as websites. There are a number or acceptable ways of constructing bibliographies and you must check which is most suitable for your particular needs.

The other way of referencing other people's work is in your text.

Following the quote or idea you should include the author, date and page number (if applicable). The full details can then be put in a bibliography or footnote. Here are two different ways to include references directly within your text:

... as claimed by Thoreau (1993, p.7)

*or*

... an American thinker (Thoreau 1993:7) once claimed that ...

You could also use footnotes as a way of including the author, date and page number information rather than places the information in brackets. Check which referencing convention is most appropriate for your needs.

# Communicating using email

Electronic mail, or email, is a system on the Internet which allows you to send messages and other computer files to any other user who has a computer connected to the Internet. When your computer is not connected to the Internet, the incoming messages are stored by your internet service provider (ISP).

The ISP has a computer which links you to the Web. You connect your computer to your ISP using a modem and a special phone number. Your computer will have an icon for dial-up connections. Click on this icon to dial into your ISP and check your email. You may need to enter a password. At work, college or school your computers may be permanently connected to the Internet.

An email program is computer software which lets you exchange messages with other users connected to the Internet. You can normally use it for these functions:

- Prepare and store messages before sending
- Send messages to other users
- Send messages to groups of users
- Receive messages from other users
- Scan and read the messages received
- Send a reply to any message
- Print out messages onto paper
- Send and receive computer files with messages
- Delete or store messages
- Store favourite email addresses

Email can be used to send and receive text, pictures, videos and sound. With some software packages it is even possible to make phone calls to another user who has similar equipment. All email programs work in the same general way and have the following basic features:

- **Header** is where you enter the email address of the person to get the message, anyone who is to get a copy, the subject of the message.

**Online** means connected to the Internet.
**Offline** means not connected to the Internet.

**Email programs**
Eudora
Outlook
cc:Mail
Hotmail/Webmail

- **The body** is where you type the text of the message. You can cut and paste text from elsewhere, such as a word processor.
- **Address book** is where you can store the email addresses of people you know.
- **Signature** automatically adds your chosen signature and other details at the end of the message.
- **Reply options** let you return a message to the sender without typing in the email address.
- **Reply to all** lets you return your message to the sender plus anyone who was on the copy list.
- **Forward** lets you pass the email on to someone new, perhaps adding a comment of your own.

*Creating an email with attachments*

### Compose your messages offline

If you are paying for your connection time, it is best to write your messages offline, before you go online. You can then take your time and prepare several messages which are stored temporarily in your outbox. When you go online the email software can quickly send mail from your outbox and will get any mail which is waiting for you. New mail will appear in your inbox.

### *Sending email*

- Select the command or icon for a new message.
- Use the **To** field to enter the email address you want to use. This address might be available from the address book icon at the top of the screen.
- Use the **cc** field if you are sending anyone a copy.
- Use the **Subject** box for your choice of short title.
- Use the body area to type your message. You can also use the paste command to import any clip art or other effects.
- To attach a file, use the appropriate command or icon then point to the place in your computer where the file is saved.
- When finished, use the **Send** command. If you are online the email will be sent. If you are offline the email will be sent next time you go online.

### Receiving email

- Make sure you are online. For home computing this normally means selecting the icon of your internet service provider (ISP).
- The modem will dial your ISP and you may have to enter your password.
- Once you are online, use the appropriate command to download any messages from your mailbox held at the ISP.
- Any income mail is downloaded to your inbox; click on any new messages to open them.
- Read the message and perhaps reply by selecting **Reply**.
- Exit the message then transfer it from your inbox to a storage folder.

## Email addresses

There are many millions of people on the Internet and there are many possible email addresses. You need to be careful when reading and writing an address you have been given. Although they may seem confusing, email addresses always follow the same pattern:

- **User name:** this is your personal address. It could also be two names separated by a dot such as jim.jones or an underscore such as mary_jones.
- **Separator:** found on your keyboard, sometimes called the 'at' or 'axon' symbol.
- **Domain name:** an organisation has to register their particular name.
- **Type of domain:** helps to indicate the type of organisation, such as business, government, network and educational.

## Netiquette

Etiquette means good manners, netiquette means good manners on the net. If you are emailing a stranger it is wiser to be polite, just as you would with a letter or phone call. Some suggestions:

- Don't shout with capital letters.
- Always fill the **Subject** field with a helpful title.
- When replying, don't return the whole of a message.
- Check the address before you hit **Send** or **Reply**.
- Wait and think before you reply.

Messages can cause embarrassment if they reach the wrong people or fail to arrive with the right people. You cannot recall emails once they are sent.

**Common email abbreviations**

| | |
|---|---|
| AFAIK | as far as I know |
| BBL | be back later |
| BTY | by the way |
| FAQ | frequently asked questions |
| IMHO | in my humble opinion |
| RTFM | read the flipping manual |
| TTFN | tat ta for now |

**Types of domain**

| | |
|---|---|
| .com | commercial |
| .org | non-commercial |
| .gov | government |
| .edu | educational |
| .net | network |
| .co.uk | UK commercial |

**Emoticons**

| | |
|---|---|
| :-) | happy |
| :-( | sad |
| ;-) | wink |
| :-0 | shock |

# Making yourself clear

Whatever you're writing, try to make yourself clear. Develop an extensive vocabulary, a good knowledge of spelling and a solid grounding in grammar. Use punctuation in the right places.

One person's lucid shorthand is another person's gobbledygook.

### Tackling technical terms

Don't be afraid of technical terms; just learn what they mean and use them correctly. If you do use them, check that other people understand you. If they don't understand then explain. Explaining a technical term is a good opportunity to clarify your own thinking. To produce good writing, you need more than a knowledge of technical terms, but if you know the words people use it may be easier to ask for help and brush up your style.

## Grammar

Learning the rules of grammar will help to improve your communication. If you don't learn them, it probably won't stop you communicating but you may not have so much confidence in drafting your documents and presentations. Learn how to make effective use of the following:

- Nouns
- Pronouns
- Adjectives
- Verbs
- Adverbs
- Conjunctions
- Prepositions
- Interjections

## Punctuation

Punctuation is about knowing how to start, how to pause and how to stop. The punctuation marks are like signposts to the reader, helping them through your text without getting lost. Use punctuation to make your meaning clear or to achieve a special effect. If you are using a lot of punctuation, take some of it out. If your writing still makes sense then the punctuation was probably unnecessary. If your writing no longer makes sense or is ambiguous, try rewriting your sentences in a different way. Here are the punctuation marks you need to use effectively:

- Comma
- Colon
- Full stop
- Semicolon
- Dash
- Question mark
- Exclamation mark

# Spelling

Spelling mistakes are often distracting and they can even change one word into another, altering the meaning of a sentence. Most people's drafts contain a few spelling mistakes. The important thing is to proof-read your work and correct it.

---

**ENGLISH IS A LIVING LANGUAGE**

English is a living language and new words are being coined all the time. Feedback was once a technical term used by control engineers but everyone uses it now.

---

# Part 2: The Bottom Line

This part concentrates on what you must do to get your key skills qualification. It will show you:

- The words and ideas of the key skills.
- The definition of level 3.
- How you can practise the skills.
- What must be in your portfolio of evidence.

This part is divided into three sections:

- **What the unit expects**: This section will explain the evidence requirements of the communication key skill, and how to put your portfolio together. Your portfolio is the key to getting your key skill – this part of the book tells you how to choose your evidence and get it ready.
- **Evidence for level 3**
- **Other forms of assessment and evidence**: This section will tell you about the external assessment and how to prepare for it.

## Qualifications and Curriculum Authority

The key skills specifications are published by the QCA, and are widely available through schools, colleges, training establishments and awarding bodies. They are also available on the QCA website (www.qca.org.uk).

# What the unit expects

## What does complex mean?

**Complex**
complicated
involved
convoluted
intricate
not straightforward

Communicating about complex subjects is a key feature of level 3. The word 'complex' is used to identify the standard expected of you. Not only do you have to meet the demands made by the key skill requirements, you have to deal with complex subject matter. By asking you to deal with complex subjects and topics, the key skill becomes more demanding and is seen as being at a suitable standard, equivalent to A levels or Advanced GNVQs. The good news is that by working on complex topics, you will get an opportunity to use a variety of skills and techniques to help you fill your portfolio. Whatever you're doing, you should be able to find something complex.

## What is level 3 all about?

**Evidence** is the proof that you can do what is required in order to get the key skills. It is proof that you have learned about communication and that you can use and apply what you have learned.

At level 3 you will see there are four types of evidence you need to provide. You need to show you can apply your communication skills to generate evidence to prove you can:

- Discuss
- Present
- Read for information
- Write documents

# What about your portfolio?

## Building your portfolio of evidence

You portfolio of evidence is the work you have done that will prove to your teacher and others that you can do what the key skill asks you to do. It is the proof you will need to get the key skill award.

A key skill unit is quite a large amount of work. It is roughly the same size as a GNVQ unit or an A level module. So you may have to carry out a number of different tasks to have sufficient evidence to show you can meet the key skill requirements. Make sure your portfolio is well organised and that the work inside is clear and easily understood.

The simplest approach to collecting and keeping your evidence is to have a separate folder or portfolio for your communication evidence. This is by far the easiest way to organise your work and to keep a record of what you have done and what's still to be done. Consider the following ways to organise and label your work:

- Have a contents page that you keep updating as you build up your evidence.
- Keep records of when you collected your evidence and where it came from (e.g. which A level or GNVQ unit).
- Get into the habit of writing down the purpose of your work as you collect evidence.
- Use the key skill sections to divide up your portfolio.
- Copies of work are acceptable if the actual key skill evidence is part of another course.
- Keep a checklist of all the things you must cover in your portfolio (e.g. in the presenting section you must show you can use an image).

# Evidence for level 3

### Complex points

A complex point is simply a complicated line of reasoning or a complicated argument that others will find potentially difficult to understand. The key skill is looking to see how you handle these difficult ideas or points when you explain them to others. You are expected to help others understand complex points by putting your communication skills to work to simplify the points using appropriate communication techniques. For example, you could adapt detailed sales figures or trends to represent them on a graph to help others understand what has happened. You might help others understand what you mean by using figures of speech in your explanations, or by explaining something using a context the group will be more familiar with.

## Taking part in discussions

### Background information

This part of the key skill is asking you to show that you can be an active participant in discussions. The key skill is trying to see whether you can contribute in discussions and participate in other ways as well. This means contributing, listening, encouraging other people, helping to involve other people.

### What you must learn to do

### Make a contribution

- **Contributing effectively:** your contributions need to be clear and relevant to the discussion. Check you have made yourself understood. If your contribution involves a complicated argument, use techniques to help people understand it then check how much they have taken in.
- **Adapting to circumstances:** it is not enough just to be clear and relevant. You also need to show you can suit the circumstances. Your contribution should be appropriate for the group and the topic. For example, it may be a formal gathering or an informal group; keep this in mind and adapt your contributions accordingly. The topic

under discussion may be sensitive and your contributions should be suitably phrased. If it is a serious topic then being flippant or insincere is failing to acknowledge the nature of the topic and may be offending those in the group who intend to treat it seriously.

- **Coping with rejection:** try not to react if your argument or opinion is not accepted by others or is not treated properly by others. This is someone else showing that they are not able to participate effectively. Respond politely, and let it go.

### *Listen and respond*

- **Listening to others:** even when you are not talking, you still need to be working to earn this part of the key skill. You need to show that you are an active listener, paying attention to what others say and showing that you are receptive to their contributions. There are several ways you can do this but the most obvious is to ask questions. When you ask questions, take account of what other people have said. Be attentive.

- **Responding appropriately:** acknowledge any gender or cultural considerations; show that you are aware of how others might be feeling. This could involve acknowledging that others are uncomfortable about certain topics or certain aspects of the discussion; it could involve taking appropriate action or simply showing you are aware of other people's feelings. If they are nervous you could help to put them at ease or try not add to their nervousness. This means showing a little empathy towards others in the group.

**Attentive:** to be alert and pay attention to what others are saying.

**Empathy:** an awareness of how others are feeling.

### *Develop points and ideas*

You could develop points through questioning. You are showing how your contributions help to keep the discussion moving forward and help to explore the different viewpoints that exist.

### *Encourage other people*

Encourage other people by involving them in the discussion. Encourage them to continue their contributions by asking follow-up questions to help them develop their points. You could even ask someone for their opinion. Be careful not to focus attention on someone who will not welcome it. Only ask those who you think will respond positively to the encouragement.

## Collecting evidence

All examples are designed to get you to start thinking about what you need to do. You will be able to add in more information based on your own circumstances.

| HOW TO GET YOUR EVIDENCE | | |
| --- | --- | --- |
| *What you need to do* | *A topical discussion* | *Using team meetings* |
| Show you can contribute to a group discussion about a complex subject effectively. This will involve taking part in the discussion and adapting your contribution to suit the circumstances. | One of the most difficult aspects of the discussion aspect of the key skill is producing appropriate evidence. Normally your teacher will observe you. However, you can help in producing important supporting evidence by making sure you have notes on your preparation and research of the topic, your prepared questions and comments, a brief description of the topic, time and place plus the people taking part. | When you use team meetings as an opportunity to generate evidence for group discussions, concentrate on the agenda items where decisions need to be taken. Make sure there is plenty of time for a full discussion. |
| You will need to show you can listen and reply to other members of the group, demonstrating that you can respond to them appropriately. | Add to these notes during the discussion by recording key contributions from other people (a good way of showing you are listening). | Keep any records from the meeting (agenda, notes, etc.) and make sure someone is taking full minutes of the meeting. You can use the records and minutes as evidence in your portfolio. Annotate them with your own comments to help explain what communication evidence the records deal with. |
| Show you can help the discussion by developing points and ideas. | Have a reminder of the type of evidence and skills you need to show. For example, listening and responding, expanding on points and ideas, encouraging others to get involved, adopting a suitable style and contribution to match the circumstances. | Make your own notes about the seating arrangements, who's who, key decision points, who said what and notes on the points you want to make. |
| You also need to show you can encourage and involve other people in the discussion. | These are good ways of making sure you have useful supporting evidence. | |

## Evidence requirements in a nutshell

Take part in a discussion about something complicated with a group of others. It can be anything as long as it is not something that is relatively simple and straightforward. During the discussion you must show that you can make clear and relevant contributions. Avoid making irrelevant or confused contributions.

Even when you are not talking, show you can participate by listening to other people, being receptive to their contributions and answering their questions appropriately. You must show that you are aware of other people's feelings and that you can help the discussion move forward by developing some of the points and ideas shared within the group. You must also encourage others to participate by creating suitable openings.

## HINTS ON DISCUSSIONS

- Write down a brief paragraph about the context of the discussion. Include things like make-up of the group, topic under discussion, time and date.
- Try not to dominate the group with your contributions. You might be succeeding in one aspect but you will be failing in others.
- Prepare for the discussion by doing some research into the topic and making notes on the points you want to discuss or questions you might like the group to address.

# Making presentations

## Background information

Part 1 considered some ways to make your presentation as accessible as possible. You don't have to demonstrate all these techniques. You just need to show you can identify some key concerns that will be important to your audience and then show you can take account of them when you make your presentation.

Practice is the key to presenting. You are not expected to develop presentation skills overnight or meet the requirements at the first attempt. Take time to develop the necessary skills. Practise and rehearse on your own or with friends. The more presentations you do, the better you will become. This is how you gain confidence and experience. So practise and try out different techniques in different situations. Try to look for opportunities to develop your skill by making small-scale presentations in a range of circumstances. Even if you practise by doing just one or two minutes, this will help you gain confidence. Practise techniques like eye contact, voice quality and how you stand.

Start simply with brief presentations about straightforward topics then build up your skills from there. This will also allow you to practise using visual aids like OHTs. Try using just one OHT to begin with.

## What you must learn to do

### Prepare and structure your presentation

Make sure your presentation is suitable for the occasion and adapted to fit your purpose. A presentation about a design concept might involve some sort of graphics and strong visual images. A contribution in a debate will need to address other people's arguments and use powerful and persuasive

language. Think carefully about sharing any results, so the information is communicated in a clear and interesting way. Organise your presentation so other people can follow it easily and recognise your key messages.

### Adapt your style to subject and audience

Use technical language only when it's relevant and always explain it clearly to the audience. Try to avoid slang and words that are needlessly complicated or showy. Always check your understanding of difficult vocabulary and consider using a thesaurus to identify alternatives that may help more people to understand. A thesaurus is also useful to help you create alternative ways to explain complex points or ideas.

### Keep your audience interested

Don't fill your presentation with millions of attention-grabbing devices. Develop your overall skills then choose a few techniques that will suit your subject and your audience. Your presentation doesn't have to be very long, so bear that in mind when you're choosing.

You are expected to use at least one image to illustrate or explain a complex point. This means working the image into your presentation and showing that you can use it effectively. The key skill is encouraging you to be a versatile communicator, adapting to different circumstances by using different techniques and tools.

## Collecting evidence

| HOW TO GET YOUR EVIDENCE | | |
|---|---|---|
| *What you need to do:* | *Marketing Brand X* | *Making a proposal* |
| Present a complex subject, showing you can speak clearly and organise what you say, making it easy for others to follow.<br><br>Use at least one image to help you make your presentation. Also show you can use a range of other techniques to keep the audience interested.<br><br>Show you can adapt your presentation to suit your:<br>• Purpose<br>• Subject<br>• Audience<br>• Situation | **Time**: about 6 minutes<br><br>**When**: Friday afternoon (3 pm)<br><br>**Group**: 8 class members doing similar work for their business course.<br><br>**Visual aids**<br>I have three OHTs (one is a table and one is a pie chart to be used to show some market research, the last one outlines my proposed strategy). Using an overhead projector might also help me hold the group's interest more on a Friday afternoon. OHTs to be given out as handouts at the end. Hopefully, it will also help me keep the interest level high and keep the group focused on a Friday afternoon. | **Time:** 8 minutes<br><br>**Group**: chair, minute secretary, 10 team members.<br><br>Keep the agenda for the meeting and the resulting minutes as evidence for your portfolio.<br><br>**Techniques**<br>In these types of presentations I may decide it is appropriate to use a little exaggeration or hyperbole to add emphasis to a point. There will have to be a balance between being forceful, favouring one position over another, and still appearing rational, presenting my view as in the best interests of the group. |

---

**Thesaurus:** a book containing lists of words with the same or similar meanings

**Techniques to engage group**

Eye contact. I have written into the presentation lots of local references and I'm going to try to use body language for added emphasis to help reinforce what I am proposing in my marketing strategy.

*Continued on page 55*

Sincerity will be crucial and eye contact will be vital (perhaps dwelling a little longer on the people I make eye contact with, especially key team members). Sincerity can also be reflected in the tone of my voice.

I have used PowerPoint to make the presentation more colourful, striking and persuasive.

In a formal committee or team setting there are rules and etiquette that I need to follow.

## Evidence requirements in a nutshell

You need to make a presentation about a complex topic. It can be anything as long as it is not something relatively simple and straightforward. The idea is to give you a challenge so you can demonstrate a variety of techniques and skills to help the group understand your topic. You must adapt your vocabulary and style. You must organise your presentation to suit your purpose and your audience. You must use a minimum of one image during your presentation, and you must use it to explain a complex point.

### HINTS ON MAKING A PRESENTATION

- Take time to prepare your notes; you can use them as part of your evidence.
- Keep a copy of the images you use; note how, why and where you used them.
- Keep details like the time, length, topic of your presentation and what you knew about the group you were talking to. Explain how you adapted or changed things to make your presentation more effective.
- Practice with friends or family and don't be afraid to ask for advice or constructive criticism.

# Reading and synthesising information

## Background information

### How to synthesise information

Read about something using different sources of information, then draw together what you understand and use it to help you create your own

The Bottom Line

**Synthesis**
amalgamate
combine
integrate
unify
draw together
pull together

**Extended documents**
textbooks
non-fiction books
company reports
newspapers
magazines
journals
documents on the web
essays

opinion. You could say that this is having an informed opinion. Reading from different sources provides you with the knowledge and understanding you need to form your own opinion.

### What is an extended document?

Extended documents are longer documents. A document may be almost anything you read. It needn't be a book or a magazine; it could be information from the Internet, and include a collection of images. The key skill specification states that some of your extended documents must include at least one image.

## What you must learn to do

### Find relevant information

The key skill requirements focus on your abilities to skim sources of information to find the specific material you need to use. This means you need to have a clear idea what you are looking for and know how to recognise it when you see it. You are not expected to read through every word on every page. This is why the key skill uses words like 'scanning' and 'skimming'. You are expected to locate what you need to know in a quick and efficient way.

### Use sources of reference

When confronted with complex ideas, arguments or information, you must use appropriate sources of reference and support to help you understand what is being said. It doesn't matter whether you ask someone for clarification, or go to other sources, as long as you use the support available to you. Sources of reference include dictionaries, encyclopedias (on paper, websites and CD-ROMs), databases, books and journals.

### Detect opinion and bias

You need to show you can detect any prejudice or bias in your sources. Do they favour one version of events, or support one argument or position over another? How does this influence what they say? You need to be objective when you read your sources. Make up your own mind or form your own opinion when you feel that you have a full grasp of different accounts. Check your understanding of what you've read. The sources of information may be written from a subjective viewpoint and favour one point over another. In a mild form this is an opinion, but when an opinion is pushed more heavily and not all the facts are taken into account, you might be dealing with bias. Make sure you can recognise it.

### Synthesise your information

Develop an informed opinion about what you read and present it in your own way. You could be writing a report or essay, talking to a group or making notes to help you prepare for a discussion.

## WHAT YOU MUST LEARN TO DO IN A NUTSHELL

- Use two appropriate information sources.
- Quickly zoom in on the information you need.
- Use other sources to help check your understanding.
- Spot any bias and compare different sources.
- Draw together and use information from different sources.

## Collecting evidence

### HOW TO GET YOUR EVIDENCE

| What you need to do | Marketing Brand X Continued from page 53 | Researching an essay |
|---|---|---|
| Generate text about a complex subject based on your understanding of appropriate information taken from two extended documents.<br><br>One of the documents must have at least one relevant image.<br><br>Make sure your work shows you understood and compared the different arguments, lines of reasoning and main points of text and images.<br><br>Draw together what you have learned from both documents into a single form that can be used for a specific purpose, e.g. a report or presentation. | I could use a company annual report and a newspaper or magazine article on the company's performance for that year.<br><br>I will need to zoom in on the information I need and be aware of any bias or opinion.<br><br>I will use a book on marketing basics to help me understand some of the concepts and terms in my two main sources.<br><br>*Continued on page 57* | I could look at two authors with different perspectives about the same historical event. Perhaps they have different opinions about why something happened. I'm going to compare accounts.<br><br>I can gather other information to help me understand key concepts from encyclopedias, CD-ROMs and the Internet.<br><br>I will create an accurate account of the two authors' arguments, comparing their positions. I will also try to use these sources to have my own informed opinion on what I have studied. |

## Evidence requirements in a nutshell

You have to take what you've learned about a complex subject from two different sources and pull it together into a piece of your own. This can be a presentation, an essay or anything else that has a clear purpose. You must show you can read sources to locate relevant information. Use at least one image. Interpret your information by comparing different accounts. Recognise opinions, arguments and bias.

**HINTS ON READING FOR INFORMATION**

- Focus on a complex subject that generates different opinions.
- Keep records of sources and evidence.
- Note authors, titles, publishers, dates, ISBNs.
- Maybe quote a few passages that are particularly telling.
- Comment on the opinions, political position, bias or beliefs.
- Note down your thoughts and explain how you arrived at them.

# Writing documents

## Background information

This aspect of the key skill requires you to produce two different types of document about complex subjects. One of the documents must be an extended document including at least one image.

Effective writing communicates with the reader; it normally uses simple words to convey one meaning that is easy to understand. Here are some guidelines:

- Use a document style that suits your information
- Organise your document to be clear and consistent
- Follow standard grammar, spelling and punctuation
- Break up your text using well-chosen images

Level 3 requires you to produce two different types of document about complex subjects. One of them must contain an image and it must be an extended document. You can treat 'extended' as meaning more than three pages of A4 but don't focus on the minimum requirements. Find a way to enjoy working on your document and produce something people will want to read. The other document could be:

- A formal letter
- A set of instructions
- A leaflet or brochure
- A newspaper article
- Some display material
- A handout for a presentation

You can also use electronic material as long as you show it's your own work.

## What you must learn to do

### Select an appropriate style and form

You need to show that you can make decisions about how to present your work effectively. Choose a style that suits your subject and your audience.

Vocabulary, sentence structures and tone can all be adapted to suit your reader and your purpose. They can also be adapted to suit the sensitivity of your subject. Look at how tabloids and broadsheets present the same news story. Newspapers adapt the news to suit their readers and sell more copies.

### Take relevant information and present it clearly

You are being asked to show appropriate organisation of your written material. This means making effective use of paragraphs, headings, sub-headings, italics and highlighting. You are also required to show that you can organise your work and your thoughts. Arrange your ideas in a logi-cal order, present your arguments clearly and justify any conclusions you draw. Be aware of any weaknesses in your reasoning, any counter-arguments that exist or any alternative interpretations you could reach.

Remember that you trying to communicate a complex subject in a clear piece of writing. It is often harder to explain something by using everyday language than by using technical terms. But it is well worth the attempt; the results can be very rewarding. If the people reading your work are fam-iliar with the subject and its technical vocabulary, then it may be more sen-sible to use it. You are trying to show that you can write appropriately for your audience.

### Write clear sentences with accurate spelling

Do the basics to make your text understandable. You need to form your sentences correctly and put punctuation marks in the right places.

## Collecting evidence

### HOW TO GET YOUR EVIDENCE

| What you need to do | Marketing Brand X<br>Continued from page 55 | Extended essay |
|---|---|---|
| You need to show that you can write two different types of document about complex subjects. One has to be an extended document including at least one image.<br><br>Your documents must show you can select and use an appropriate form and style of writing that suits your purpose and the subject matter. | I am trying to produce a marketing report that is as realistic as possible, so I will write it as though my intended audience is the company management. This will influence the language and style.<br><br>I have looked at professionally produced marketing reports used in industry and will base my structure on those. | The essay can be about anything. However, if it is to be an example of an extended document, it must include some sort of image. If your essay doesn't have an image, it can be used as the other document.<br><br>The structure of the essay is important and you should take time to plan the essay, writing out the intended structure and the key concepts to be covered. |

| What you need to do | Marketing Brand X | Extended essay |
|---|---|---|
| Make sure that you organise the relevant information clearly and coherently, using any specialist language appropriately.<br><br>Your meaning must be clear and your text must be legible. Spelling, grammar and punctuation must also be accurate. | I will produce it on computer, integrating into the text the graphs I need. I can create the graphs using a spreadsheet package.<br><br>I will use a computer spellchecker then I will print out drafts and check their grammar and punctuation. | Concentrate on having a clear introduction that establishes an appropriate tone. You need to sort out how you intend to organise and present your research and thoughts.<br><br>Plan the body of your text to ensure your information and ideas will be clear and easy to follow. Make sure your points are clearly explained and justified.<br><br>Think about your conclusion when you are planning. Make sure you re-emphasise key points and arguments then draw the work together. Concentrate on planning a strong finish.<br><br>Check the specialist language; check your spelling, grammar and punctuation; and check you have a consistent tone and style. |

## Evidence requirements in a nutshell

Produce two written documents. One of them must be quite long and it must contain an image. The other must be a different type of document. Make sure that both documents suit your purpose, subject and audience.

Make sure your information is organised into clear and appropriate structures. Use technical language correctly and give the right explanation for your audience. Check your grammar, punctuation and spelling.

## HINTS ON WRITING DOCUMENTS

- Create a plan for your work and put it in your portfolio. It can show early thoughts on oganisation and the development work you have done.
- Keep the various drafts you have made, especially the drafts that show your edits and any changes to punctuation or grammar. Don't be afraid to reveal your mistakes in early drafts because this shows you can spot them yourself.
- Print out a clean copy of your final written work to keep as a record of your finished document. This may sound a little obvious but you might be submitting a clean copy of your work as evidence for another course.
- Keep backup copies of your work when you use computers.

# Other forms of assessment and evidence

## External assessment at level 3

You will need to take an external assessment as well as produce a portfolio of communication evidence. The external assessment is designed to show that you can do communication tasks at the correct level under a different set of circumstances. You might be asked to do the assessment in a single long session or in several shorter sessions. This is up to your school, college or assessor to organise for you.

### What is the point of an external assessment?

The idea of an external assessment is that someone else sets you a series of communication tasks, then gives you all the information you need to get on with them. That way you can show that you can carry out different communication work to complete tasks set by other people. Your portfolio shows that you can use communication to carry out your own tasks.

It is also attempting to show that you can do larger, related tasks under controlled conditions, such as a time limit, and with someone else setting the tasks). Here is how to look at the portfolio and the external assessments:

- The portfolio shows that you can set your own communication tasks to meet your own deadlines and time constraints.
- The external assessments show that you can carry out larger, related communication tasks set by other people and meeting the imposed time limits.

When you meet these requirements, you will get your key skill in Communication, you will have proved that you can do the communication work under a range of different conditions and in different contexts

# Part 3: Opportunities

This part highlights opportunities for generating communication evidence in the qualifications you are taking. It will show you:

- How your qualifications can be used to generate communication evidence.
- Where the best opportunities for this evidence arise in the qualifications.

This part is divided into two sections:

- **Evidence from A-level courses**: You will find this section useful whichever awarding body you are with.
- **Evidence from Vocational A-level courses**: This section will be useful regardless of whether you are working towards a 6-unit or 12-unit award.

The examples provided should be seen as starting points for generating evidence. You will see that some qualifications provide more opportunities than others. However, all contain some opportunities and will at least get you started. Make sure that you take time to read not just your subjects but also subjects that are related to the ones you are taking. This will help you gain a fuller understanding of how and where number evidence can be produced. For example, if you are doing a Business GNVQ then look also at the Business Studies GCSE and the Retail and Distributive Services GNVQ. You may also want to check out the Leisure and Tourism GNVQ.

### Vocational awards
The GNVQ Advanced awards are now called Vocational A-levels. From September 2001 GNVQ Foundation and Intermediate awards are likely to be known as Vocational GCSEs.

# Evidence from A-level courses

## Art A-level

### About the syllabus

The Art awards aim to combine intellectual and creative development with analytical, experimental and technical skills. They also aim to develop aesthetic understanding and critical judgement. The programmes of learning are intended to give you an appreciation of the interconnectedness of art, craft and design and their roles in different societies and cultures, both contemporary and historical.

*See also:* **Art and Design Vocational A-level**, page 92.

## Topic area 1
## Personal studies and investigations

### Discussions

Personal studies and investigations give you the opportunity to do what you want with the media and materials with which you want to work. The production of an art, craft or design outcome is a substantial and complex activity that will need to be broken down into a series of discrete tasks.

As you prepare to explore and experiment with ideas, media and materials, you will need to plan and organise. You are not expected to do this alone. You can discuss your ideas with:

- Your tutor
- Other people on your programme
- Members of any team you are in
- Artists, craftspeople or designers
- Librarians, gallery assistants, etc.

Each discussion will need to be considered carefully so you can get the best out of it. This will involve:

- Selecting the correct approach and choosing the right moment
- Listening to what others say and responding constructively
- Knowing how to use questions, pauses and body language

### Presentation

Some artists, craftspeople and designers are unwilling to discuss or present their work to others because they believe it speaks for itself.

Increasingly, these views are outmoded as galleries, museums, collectors and patrons expect creative individuals not only to know what they are doing and be able to do it, but also to be able to explain it intelligibly to others.

Your presentation may come at the end of your work but it may also take place as part of your interim review in the middle of your project. The timing of your presentation should have no impact on its quality, only on what you present and how you present it. You should:

- Decide what you want to do in your presentation, i.e. present your initial drawings, sketches or models or your response to a design brief.
- Be clear about who your audience is and at what level to pitch your presentation. If you are speaking to a familiar audience comprising your peers, you may be more relaxed in tone and formality than if you are dealing with a collector, client or patron.
- Always use a structure to help your audience follow what you are saying. You can do this by preparing your drawings, designs or slides in an order that will remind you of your development, or by having a set of notes to help you.
- Use a range of presentation techniques to make sure you hold the audience's attention. In addition to your visual work, this could include asking and answering questions, demonstrations of methods or techniques, or simply the way you talk to them using specialist language and an engaging manner.

### Reading for information

Your creative development and achievement will depend upon the quality of your exploration and research as well as on your skill and creativity. You will need to explore, evaluate and synthesise a range of sources if you are to:

- Choose your media, materials, technology and equipment
- Investigate different genres, styles and techniques for your work
- Understand the variety of ways to present your final outcomes

These sources will include:

- Text and reference books
- Specialist magazines and articles
- Original works and gallery publications
- Technical manuals and specifications
- Specialist websites and CD-ROMs

Your communication skills will help you to:

- Locate and skim sources to select relevant items
- Scan the selected items to read and review the information
- Verify your interpretation and understanding with others
- Check one source against another to test its accuracy
- Record things for future use in your sketchbook, notebook or visual log

### Writing documents

People do not always realise the contribution that their visual work can make to the key skill of communication. Certainly in terms of evidence, it is unlikely that your visual work could be described as an extended document. However, there is an opportunity for your outcomes to:

- Contribute to an extended document
- Provide evidence about complex subjects

Your work may provide an alternative form of written evidence; here are two possibilities:

- Drawings, sketches, illustrations or photographs of your personal study, together with your notes or other written descriptions of your studies and investigations and final outcome
- Individual pieces of work that are carefully analysed and evaluated using the appropriate conventions for writing

## Topic area 2
## Fine art

### Discussion

For many people fine art is the only form they recognise; in their view, all art is fine art. As someone working in this specialist area and who has chosen fine art as a topic, you will be expected not only to have a view on what fine art is, but also to:

- Explain what you mean by fine art to others
- Demonstrate fine art through your work
- Recognise fine art in other people's work.

This is not as easy as it seems because the boundaries between art, craft and design are blurred, just as the scope of the topic is broad. At one time it was possible simply to look at an individual's work and say whether it was fine art, ceramics, textiles, photography, graphic design, and so on. Increasingly, individuals work in a range of different areas and media, so it is difficult to decide whether the classification follows the artist or the context.

For example, is David Hockney a fine artist? If so, is everything he does to be classified as fine art whether he is using photography to record images or providing costumes and stage design for the theatre? Or is he a fine artist, a photographer, a costume designer and set designer? Does it matter?

You will be expected to discuss your ideas about fine art with individuals and others. You will learn to use your speaking and listening skills to develop your knowledge and understanding and use them to benefit your visual work.

### Presentation

Fine art outcomes are traditionally presented in exhibitions. These can be:

- Within your school or college

- At a local venue such as a community centre
- In a public space such as a museum or library
- In a private space such as a commercial gallery
- At an outside site
- On the Internet

Presenting your final work can be a very stressful occasion. Prepare properly to improve your chances of success:

- Check out the venue beforehand and ensure the facilities are adequate. Look at the room space, the electricity supply and the socket locations. Make sure the venue is safe for you and your audience.
- Think through what you want to say about your work and the best words and expressions to use, either in an exhibition catalogue or when talking to others.
- Decide how you want to present, display or exhibit your work. This should be done to help others understand and make your meaning clear. It may involve you in guiding people through the exhibition or directing people to look at specific works or parts of your work in a particular order.
- Use techniques to draw attention to what you see as important in your work, such as lighting or questions, or even audience participation.

### Reading for information

An exhibition, display or performance will need a lot of planning and preparation, which will require you to gather, assimilate and synthesise a wide range of information effectively. This may involve you in reading:

- Gallery notes and plans that include measurements
- Contracts and hire details that include fees, times and dates
- Transport and other organisational details
- Technical documents on health and safety or insurance

You may also need to proof-read notes or a catalogue for your own exhibition. A successful exhibition will require you to interpret and assimilate many types of information and bring them together competently.

### Writing documents

An exhibition catalogue is a good example of an extended document on a complex subject and including a range of images. If you are not responsible for the whole document (i.e. if it is for a group exhibition or the exhibition is being organised by other people) your personal section in it could provide some evidence for the communication key skill, especially if it contains:

- An illustration showing one of your images
- Your biographical information
- Lists of other works with details of medium and size of materials
- A personal statement on your work
- Your views on fine art

**What you must know**
Part 1: The Learning Curve will help you with the knowledge you need.

**What you must do**
Part 2: The Bottom Line will help you with the evidence you need.

**Opportunities**

### Further opportunities for evidence

Although personal investigations and fine art are explored in detail here, processes, ideas and methods are equally relevant to other specialist areas covered by the Art A-level specifications, including:

- 3D design
- Graphics
- Textiles
- Photography.

# Biology A-level

### About the syllabus

The Biology award aims to develop essential knowledge and understanding in biology and how to use them in new and changing situations. It will also help you to develop an understanding of scientific methods and the contribution of new technology, particularly information and communication technology.

*See also:* **Science Vocational A-level**, page 123.

## Topic area 1
## Working on your experimental skills

### Discussion

You will have the opportunity to formulate a clear plan, carry out your experiments, record your results and evaluate your work. When planning and carrying out investigations you are expected to:

- Identify the question or problem using available information
- Choose working procedures that are safe and effective
- Select appropriate apparatus, materials and organisms
- Consider what might be fruitful measurements and observations
- Be aware of safety, ethics and the environment

Consult other people when you analyse the problem, choose your equipment and decide on interpretation and recording. Your programme of study will give you the opportunity to discuss these important aspects with:

- Your tutor
- Other people on your programme
- Members of any team you are in
- Specialists on the organisms you study

To take advantage of the discussion opportunities to increase your knowledge and understanding and to take the investigation forward, you should:

- Share your ideas and thoughts on the problem
- Acknowledge that other people may have valid ideas
- Be prepared to listen and learn from others; encourage quiet members of the group to contribute their views
- Listen to everyone, even the shyest person

## Presentation

While executing your experiments or investigations you will be expected to use apparatus and materials correctly and safely, and work in a methodical and organised way. You may have the opportunity to demonstrate or present your experiment to others. This is a very important skill in both biology and communication.

When you are demonstrating experimental skills or an investigation you should:

- Prepare and test the apparatus, equipment or organisms in advance
- Make sure your audience can see and hear everything
- Provide yourself with aids such as notes or illustrations
- Match your descriptions to what is happening in the demonstration
- Explain any technical language or specialist terms you use
- Draw attention to key points or changes in behaviour
- Record appropriate observations and measurements to a degree of precision agreed with your tutor

## Reading for information

While preparing for experiments or when investigating a particular question or problem, you will be expected to use secondary sources such as textbooks, articles and reports to:

- Analyse biological information and ideas
- Interpret technical data including statistics
- Understand line graphs, histograms, annotated drawings and diagrams

The assimilation and synthesis of this information from a variety of sources will involve:

- Skimming your sources to select the most relevant
- Scanning your selections and recording useful items
- Examining your items to uncover trends or patterns
- Cross-referring to other sources or with your tutor
- Distilling the essentials to help you make progress

## Writing documents

Communicating the findings or results of your experimental and investigative activities using biological knowledge and understanding will require you to select and use appropriate methods to:

- Describe the processes
- Analyse the outcomes
- Present the conclusions
- Illustrate the outcomes
- Use data to show trends
- Use data to make comparisons
- Evaluate evidence and procedures

Your outcomes will produce a range of information. You can demonstrate effective writing skills by:

Opportunities

- Organising this diverse material into a logical, coherent document
- Linking diagrams, texts and numbers to support your conclusions
- Writing clearly using accurate grammar, punctuation and spelling

## Topic area 2
## Preparing for your practical examinations

Practical examinations will build on your experience, knowledge and techniques developed during your work on experimental skills. The examinations will try to determine how well you can carry out the process on your own. In preparing and practising for this task, you will have the opportunity to develop and apply a range of skills that will produce authentic evidence for your communication key skill.

### *Discussion*

The nature of this topic means that your oral skills will have little or no opportunity to be used beyond:

- Seeking advice from others
- Practising in trial situations

The most important contribution that your speaking and listening skills can make will be to help you to seek the correct advice and ask relevant questions as you build up your confidence and capability in practical work.

### *Reading for information*

Your reading skills will help you to revise and review past work as you prepare for the examination. The sort of material you should be reading will comprise:

- Your own records of past experiments and investigations
- Past examination papers and model experiments
- Textbooks, revision aids and revision guides
- Information sources that are not solely text-based

Different people attempt to synthesise their understanding in different ways. These include producing:

- Detailed written notes
- Full copies of the information read
- Tapes produced by dictation
- Electronic notes and records
- Flow charts, spider diagrams, etc.

The important point is to find a method that works for you.

### *Writing documents*

Your practical work will produce results that should be recorded in a form that can be analysed, interpreted, explained and communicated in a way that justifies your original hypothesis. This process will include:

- Analysing evidence

- Making reliable observations
- Making accurate measurements
- Presenting observations and calculations
- Identifying trends and patterns in data

You are expected to draw this information together, record and use it to provide conclusions and an evaluation. Your evaluation should include:

- A critical analysis of experimental techniques
- Charts, diagrams, graphs and tables to present findings
- An explanation of the trends and patterns identified

You should produce an extended document that organises this information into a coherent report. Your findings and evaluations should be illustrated with appropriate data and images. Do not undermine the quality of your experimental practice by failing to apply the fundamental principles of grammar, punctuation and spelling.

### Further opportunities for evidence

The Biology A-level has a specific requirement for you to generate key skill evidence through the quality of your written communication.

**What you must know**
Part 1: The Learning Curve will help you with the knowledge you need.

**What you must do**
Part 2: The Bottom Line will help you with the evidence you need.

# Business Studies A-level

### *About the syllabus*

The Business Studies award aims to develop an understanding of organisations, the markets they serve and the process of adding value. It will help you to understand business behaviour from the customer, manager, creditor, owner and employee perspectives and it will improve your own decision-making and problem-solving skills. It will give you the opportunity to develop and apply the full range of your communication skills.

### Topic area 1
### Marketing

*See also:* **Business Vocational A-level**, page 96.

### *Discussion*

You will need to understand how a business behaves as it looks first to find then satisfy customers. You will be expected to find information on:

- The market for your chosen business
- Its market research techniques
- Its approach to marketing planning
- Relevant accounting and finance

Your programme of study will give you an opportunity to discuss these topics with:

- Your tutor
- Other people on your programme
- Business specialists

Opportunities

When using speaking and listening skills to find out information from others, you should:

- Be clear about the topics you wish to discuss
- Understand the fundamentals of what you are discussing
- Use appropriate specialist terms or technical language
- Prepare questions in advance about key areas
- Ask relevant questions at relevant moments
- Ask for clarification when you need it
- Always be polite and encourage other people to participate
- Know how to record important information you've obtained

### Presentation

You may be asked to research a particular strand of marketing and present your findings to others on your programme. These strands may include:

- The nature and role of marketing
- Market research methods
- Marketing plans
- Forecasting

Finding out about market research may involve a practical exercise in which you apply market research techniques to collect data on customer attitudes and needs. This data will enable you to present your findings by:

- Preparing detailed statistical evidence
- Producing charts and tables on customer responses
- Showing how the data identifies changing customer needs
- Using the data to revise forecasting figures and pricing strategies

Check that your audience is following the main points of your presentation. You can do this by asking questions at appropriate points or by responding to questions from the audience.

### Reading for information

Not all the information you require can be collected from others or from practical activities. You will also need to develop the ability to research, evaluate, select, assimilate and synthesise information from a range of sources. Typical sources will include:

- Reference books and textbooks
- Reports and records of meetings
- Market research documents
- Websites and CD-ROMs

Your challenge will be to:

- Identify useful sources through skimming
- Extract relevant information by scanning
- Select and record useful and objective information
- Confirm your understanding through discussion
- Assimilate your findings and draw conclusions

### Writing documents

Your research should provide you with a clear understanding of market behaviour, in particular the potential for growth and its financial implications. Your research evidence will give you the opportunity to produce an extended illustrated document on marketing. This document should:

- Combine your writing with statistical and graphical evidence
- Use appropriate technical terms and expressions
- Use all forms of evidence to greatest effect, including images
- Comply with the requirement for accurate use of language

## Topic area 2
## Accounting and finance

### Discussion

You will need to demonstrate how accounting and financial information is used to assist decision making and financial control and then the wider strategic objectives of a business. To do this effectively, you need to understand:

- The purpose of budgets
- The role of balance sheets
- Profit and loss accounts
- How to analyse costs

This will require you to have discussions with:

- Mathematics tutors
- Accountancy tutors
- Other students
- Business specialists

### Presentation

You may be asked to research and present information on:

- Budgeting in general
- Balance sheets
- Profit and loss accounts
- Classifying and analysing costs
- Investment factors

These strands will involve a high degree of technical language and technical discussion. Many people do not feel comfortable about discussing anything to do with numbers or mathematics, even if they are important aspects of their programme. Any presentation you make should:

- Recognise the audience and its needs
- Explain any technical terms or expressions
- Show calculations or methods more than once
- Give time for audience questions
- Help people to participate without embarrassment

### Reading for information

You are not expected to produce your own financial information or accounts but you are expected to modify the accounts of others. To do this effectively, you must have a clear understanding of the documentation. To gain this understanding, you will need to have read, reviewed, analysed and synthesised:

- How businesses use accounts
- How to interpret accounts
- How to do ratio analysis
- How to assess liquidity and profitability

Any analysis or activity involving numerical data must be carefully checked for accuracy. Understand what you are doing, make calculations to the appropriate level of accuracy, and check your work for errors.

### Writing documents

The central purpose of accounting and finance is to ensure that business decisions are made in the light of strategic objectives and shaped by financial data. Your written work must show that you understand:

- How budgets and finance are used for income and expenditure
- The difference between cash flow and profit
- How to interpret a balance sheet and profit and loss account

Use your skills to select and develop the most appropriate forms of presentation. Your written work should combine text and graphical material that provides the qualitative and quantitative information you have produced. Consider:

- Handwritten text
- The role of ICT
- Combining text, images and numbers

**What you must know**
Part 1: The Learning Curve will help you with the knowledge you need.

**What you must do**
Part 2: The Bottom Line will help you with the evidence you need.

# Chemistry A-level

### About the syllabus

The Chemistry award aims to develop essential knowledge and understanding of chemistry and how to use them in new and challenging situations. It will also help you to develop an understanding of the connection between theory and experiment and how advances in information technology and instrumentation are used in chemistry. The programme of learning will also help you to appreciate the role of scientific knowledge in society and how to use it responsibly; it will sustain and develop your enjoyment and interest in chemistry.

# Topic area 1
## Applying your knowledge and understanding

See also: **Science Vocational A-level**, page 123.

### Discussion

You will be expected to recognise, recall and understand facts, terminology, principles, concepts and practical techniques. Your programme of study will provide you with the opportunity to develop your knowledge and understanding through discussions with:

- Your tutor
- Other people on your programme
- Members of any team you are in

You should be able to make informed contributions to discussions and develop a range of topics in chemistry, including:

- Formulas and equations
- Atomic structure
- Bonding and structure
- Energetics
- Kinetics
- Equilibria
- Redox
- Inorganic chemistry
- The periodic table
- Organic chemistry

### Presentation

The discussions may sometimes take the form of a presentation in which you describe a piece of work you have done or explain a particular topic to other people. To do this effectively, you should:

- Carefully organise your knowledge and understanding
- Provide appropriate visual aids or handouts
- Explain chemical principles using specialist vocabulary
- Present arguments and ideas clearly and logically
- Use tables, graphs and diagrams to explain chemical changes
- Invite comments or questions from the audience

### Reading for information

An important skill in chemistry is your ability to balance what you find out through discussion and experimentation with information drawn from other sources. These sources will vary according to the topic but will include:

- Textbooks for basic knowledge and understanding
- Magazines, periodicals and reports for chemistry in society
- Internet and research papers for the latest scientific advances

You will be expected to extend your factual knowledge and your personal opinions on matters in chemistry through the systematic analysis and synthesis of these diverse sources. This will involve:

- Selecting relevant documents by skimming
- Selecting relevant information by scanning
- Using the information to grasp chemical ideas
- Comparing different approaches and attitudes
- Synthesising the information to make judgements

### Writing documents

All activities in chemistry require written records. These may include:

- Notes made before or after a discussion
- OHTs, slides or handouts for a presentation
- Memos or emails sent to people in a planning team
- Evaluation and synthesis of sources
- Descriptions in a laboratory notebook
- Extended reports of theoretical investigations

The evidence you present for written communication skills at this level will need to be in the form of documents about complex subject matter in order to meet the key skill requirement. You will be expected to support your written work using images. These could be:

- Diagrams or drawings of chemical processes
- Diagrams of chemical structures
- Pie charts, histograms or similar graphs

## Topic area 2
## Working on your experimental and investigative skills

### Discussion

You will be required to develop and plan an experimental and investigative activity. This is best done by breaking it down into a series of discrete tasks that use appropriate skills and techniques. This activity in chemistry should provide you with the opportunity to discuss things with other people and:

- Decide on the nature of your experiment or investigation
- Select appropriate techniques, equipment and instruments
- Agree safe working practices and procedures
- Confirm your methods of measuring and recording

When these discussions are in a group situation you can generate key skill evidence by:

- Showing you understand when and how to share your ideas with other people, such as explaining which aspect of chemistry you wish to investigate.
- Listening carefully to other people's recommendations or suggestions and responding positively by taking forward their ideas or by amending your own, such as revising a working procedure or degrees of precision for measurements.
- Encouraging others to develop a line of thought or explain further by asking supplementary questions on points of technical detail.

### Presentation

You may have the opportunity to demonstrate a practical experiment to others. This offers you a further opportunity to generate key skill evidence:

- Be adequately prepared and check all your equipment in advance
- Be confident and comfortable with what you're doing
- Be aware of what is likely to happen during your demonstration
- Conduct your demonstration safely and skilfully
- Describe your observations in appropriate technical terms
- Explain any technical terms before you start to use them
- Work logically and explain each stage to the audience
- Interpret observations so the audience can make sense of them

### Reading for information

As well as having discussions or consulting others on approaches to experimentation and investigation, you are expected to synthesise existing knowledge, principles and concepts from different areas of chemistry. To do this effectively and to the level expected, you should know how to:

- Find suitable secondary sources and identify relevant texts (skim)
- Sort and sift relevant texts for information you need (scan)
- Check one source agqinst another or ask someone else
- Make judgements on what you've read to develop your ideas

### Writing documents

Experimental and investigative work offers you an opportunity to combine your practical skills in chemistry with your written communication skills. You may produce a variety of evidence, including:

- Appropriate, methodical and precise recording of the observations and measurements made during practical work, and making sure this evidence is accurately interpreted and presented in tables, diagrams or graphs.
- An extended written document that communicates the results and conclusions of your experimental or investigative activities. These results and your conclusions should be presented clearly and logically using chemical knowledge and understanding plus appropriate technical vocabulary.

As long as your evidence is sound in terms of your chemistry programme, and as long as it follows the standard conventions of grammar, punctuation and spelling, it should meet the requirements of the communication key skill.

**What you must know**
Part 1: The Learning Curve will help you with the knowledge you need.

**What you must do**
Part 2: The Bottom Line will help you with the evidence you need.

Opportunities

# Design and Technology A-level

### About the syllabus

The Design and Technology awards aim to develop innovation, design capability, recognition of constraints and the ability to produce high-

quality products. They will provide you with the opportunity to select and apply knowledge, understanding and the skills of design production processes to a range of technological activities. They will develop a critical understanding of design and technology by drawing from contemporary and historical practices.

You will be expected to use a full range of knowledge, skills, understanding, attitudes and aptitudes. In addition, you will be expected to make informed choices about appropriate applications and uses. These skills are at the heart of the key skills of capability and confidence.

The general principles of communication identified in each topic have been designed to be relevant to each of the focus areas of design and technology:

- Product design
- Food
- Systems and control

*See also*: **Engineering Vocational A-level**, page 101; **Manufacturing Vocational A-level**, page 114.

## Topic area 1
## Product development (designing)

The area of specialisation you have chosen – product design, food or systems and control – will require you to undertake a design-and-make assignment. To do this effectively, you will need to identify, explore and analyse a range of use, needs and problems to generate sufficient information to inform the development of your design brief.

The information can be drawn from primary and secondary sources. Collecting this information will create opportunities for you to demonstrate effective communication skills, including:

- Speaking and listening skills when collecting information from primary sources such as discussions of observations or consultations with others.
- Reading and synthesising the information contained in secondary sources such as other people's data or information published by manufacturers or consumer organisations.

### Discussion

Your tutor is likely to organise discussion groups with others on your programmes or with visiting experts. These will provide you with the opportunity to collect relevant data to inform your design brief by:

- Careful and effective participation in the discussion
- Explaining ideas, posing questions and evaluating answers
- Listening to other people's ideas and helping to develop them
- Using body language and eye contact to good effect

### Presentation

Once you have collected sufficient data you will be expected to assemble, organise and use this information to generate and develop ideas about possible solutions. This is the ideal time to test out your design proposals by presenting them to others. This will involve:

- Preparing your alternative designs and/or design details so they can be effectively discussed with others. This may result in a set of diagrams, drawings, sketches, models, samples, overhead transparencies (OHTs), slides or handouts.
- Being confident about what you want to say and capable of saying it clearly, succinctly and precisely. This is likely to require technical terms to describe the characterisation of components or materials, or the use of specialist tools, equipment and processes.
- Organising your ideas and materials so that others can follow and respond to different proposals or alternative design solutions.
- Using the aids you have prepared as well as your speaking and listening skills to make sure that your audience actively contribute to the presentation through questioning, requests for clarification on the proposals, or suggestions for further design developments.

### Reading for information

Any design idea and project proposal should include an understanding of the manufacturing processes, the required maintenance and the product life. These pieces of information are likely to be drawn from a range of secondary sources, including:

- Textbooks and reference books
- Industrial or commercial publications
- Manufacturing documents
- Quality control documents
- Websites and CD-ROMs

This information is likely to be of a complex nature and drawn from a diverse range of extended documents. You will need to:

- Skim the sources you have to decide which ones may be relevant
- Scan the sources you select to find the information you want
- Check your ideas by reading other sources and asking other people
- Recognise where information is accurate, speculative or of poor quality
- Assimilate, evaluate and synthesise the information you collect
- Revise your ideas and record your revisions as evidence

### Writing documents

The strategies for developing, representing, evaluating and presenting your design ideas will need to be chosen carefully. You will be expected to communicate your ideas and information unambiguously so that others can interpret your design intentions.

Your written communication skills can be demonstrated by the way you present the complex information contained in your design brief. To be effective you should:

- Select the most appropriate form to convey ideas:
  - use text to explain design decisions
  - use diagrams to demonstrate design realisations
  - use spreadsheets for calculations
  - use graphs and tables for data
- Use clear technical language and an attractive layout
- Use conventional grammar, punctuation and spelling

Other written documents could provide the remaining evidence required for written communication, perhaps a detailed annotation of a diagram or drawing containing the information used during presentations or when synthesising sources.

## Topic area 2
## Product development (making)

### Discussion

You will be expected to develop, produce or refine a production plan that will break down the activity of production into a series of discrete tasks. Given the complexity of design decisions, you will be expected to discuss them with other people before you start to make anything.

The discussions you have with others may be used to:

- Revise the production plan in the light of others' views
- Explore and evaluate the material or equipment requirements
- Consider modifying your design after a trial or test

At each stage of the making process you may wish to discuss your progress on the production plan and consider revising deadlines or production schedules.

### Presentation

You may be given the opportunity to show other people your detailed knowledge of materials and components. This may require you to present ideas on:

- Techniques that will improve a design realisation
- How to achieve a design using a particular material
- How to achieve a design using a particular component
- The safe and skilful use of tools and technologies
- Risk assessment, hazard identification, safe working practices

### Reading for information

When preparing to carry out design solutions you must have a clear understanding of:

- How you will achieve optimum resource use
- Relationships between products, materials and processes
- The agreed scale of production and maximum output
- Health and safety issues related to implementation
- How to dispose of waste products, especially combustibles

- The potential for surplus material or useful by-products
- The costs associated with production

Each of these pieces of information contributes to the complex nature of design realisation. You will be expected to research these areas carefully and use your research to inform the making process.

### Writing documents

You are required to evaluate the outcomes of the making process. This evaluation should produce a series of written and visual records as you:

- Establish criteria and procedures for quality assurance
- Assess the impact of each aspect of the making process
- Review and revise approaches, schedules and deadlines
- Consider the effectiveness of the original work plan

Appropriately and accurately recorded, these outcomes should provide valid evidence of written communication being used to consider complex subjects and they will produce an extended document. Further evidence may be generated from these items:

- Presentation of techniques and materials
- Notes on ideas, techniques and processes
- Records of tests or performance trials
- Summaries of any findings
- Proposals for modifications
- Relevant letters, memos or emails

## Further opportunities for evidence

The two topic areas, designing and making, should each provide sufficient evidence for all components of the communication key skill. However, other projects requiring a full design-and-make activity may also provide opportunities for evidence.

The programme of study itself will provide many opportunities for you to develop and apply your communication skills. Evidence for discrete components should be recorded carefully so it can be used to support more extended activities.

# General Studies A-level

### About the syllabus

The General Studies award aims to develop your ability to integrate knowledge from a range of disciplines. You will be required to demonstrate how this combined knowledge provides you with a greater understanding of the issues studied. You will learn how to interpret information and make informed judgements based on the evidence available. It will provide you with the opportunity to think constructively, critically and logically and explore a range of different approaches to problem solving.

**What you must know**
Part 1: The Learning Curve will help you with the knowledge you need.

**What you must do**
Part 2: The Bottom Line will help you with the evidence you need.

Opportunities

You will be expected to use your skills to communicate your attitudes, ideas and solutions relating to complex subjects clearly and coherently, using an appropriate format and style. The skills and knowledge you will develop within your programme of study are essential to achieving capability and confidence in the key skill of communication.

## Topic area 1
## Preparing for your examinations

The award sets examinations in three overlapping areas:

- Science, mathematics and technology
- Culture, morality, art and humanities
- Society, politics and the economy

Each of these areas will require you to develop and extend your knowledge and understanding of the disciplines involved and how they interrelate. Various approaches may be available to you as you broaden and deepen your knowledge and begin to make connections between the disciplines. Whatever approaches you take, effective communication will be essential.

### Discussion

An effective vehicle for developing and exploring your ability to communicate ideas, beliefs or concepts is a group discussion based on a chosen topic. Here are some suggestions:

- Science, mathematics and technology: What are the moral dilemmas facing scientists in the twenty-first century?
- Culture, morality, art and humanities: Can anyone be creative and innovative or are these qualities innate?
- Society, politics and the economy: What is the real meaning and value of investing in human capital?

As there are no prior knowledge requirements for the AS and A-level programmes, any discussion on these abstract topics must be handled carefully, especially if you hold very firm views and have the ability to express them clearly. An effective discussion will require you to:

- Show that you know how and when to participate, by expressing your ideas and opinions clearly and succinctly.
- Make sure that your contributions are appropriate to the nature of the group. Do not use specialist language or quote extensively from other people's work when it is clear that members of the group are not familiar with it.
- Respond to the group's dynamics by listening to others, respecting their right to speak without interruption and acknowledging ideas, values or views that differ from yours.
- Encourage others to participate through your use of gestures, eye contact or suitably framed questions and inoffensive language.

Remember that a discussion should be an effective learning experience for everyone. Try to show through your work that you have benefited from this experience.

## Presentation

A presentation can take a variety of forms, including:

- A practical demonstration of a scientific experiment or method
- An oral and practical explanation of a mathematical principle
- A short talk on a subject, topic or theory of special interest to you
- An oral examination and evaluation of ideologies, values or ethics

The main difference between a presentation and a discussion is that you are expected to take the lead in a presentation by:

- Identifying the topic or purpose
- Deciding on visual aids and handouts
- Working out what you want to say
- Using clear and appropriate language
- Presenting ideas so they're easy to follow
- Putting your points in a logical order
- Using attractive layouts and images
- Inviting audience questions and comments

A presentation has three obvious benefits:

- You can share ideas with other people
- You can extend your understanding
- You can improve your communication skills

## Reading for information

Your programme of study expects you to access complex ideas found in diverse sources of information on attitudes, beliefs and concepts. These secondary sources of information will include:

- Textbooks or reference books
- Treatises and research papers
- Magazines, newspapers and journals
- Websites, CD-ROMs and databases

Your research will usually be topic-based and you will need to:

- Explore all sources, skim lists and search directories
- Scan for relevant texts for the information you need
- Check your ideas by reading other sources and asking other people
- Be aware of an author's intentions and any bias in their work
- Evaluate your information and use it to develop your thinking

## Writing documents

Complex ideas are considered across all aspects of the programme, so any written class work should count as evidence for your communication key skill. However, the extent of this coverage will depend upon the qual-

ity and sufficiency of your written material. Evidence could be drawn from:

- Your notes produced in advance of a discussion, together with your evaluation of its outcomes, including any changes in your attitudes, beliefs or concepts
- Your notes, summaries and the resulting synthesised information you have gathered from your research activities
- An extended essay in which you have used arguments, made judgements or evaluated evidence then presented an evaluation or analysis

## Topic area 2
## Preparing for internal assessment

### Discussion

You are required to personally research or investigate an issue or problem, drawing on your knowledge and understanding of the topics introduced over the three areas of the programme. You will need to discuss your ideas with other people before you begin this assignment. You may wish to discuss your ideas with others on your programme so that you can:

- Consider the focus of your research or investigation
- Explore approaches to the research
- Seek advice on sources and how to access them
- Decide how to record the information you collect
- Decide how to present your findings

### Presentation

Begin with these three activities:

- Discuss your initial ideas with others
- Reflect on the advice received
- Devise an action plan for your assignment

After that you may wish to confirm your thinking by presenting your thoughts to the original group or to a new audience. This audience will probably be unfamiliar with your initial ideas and how you developed them.

The structure of the presentation will be similar, irrespective of your chosen audience. However, the form of your presentation should reflect how much the audience knows about your topic:

- Give an appropriate introduction with enough background
- Devise handouts with sections for those who know a bit more

Your delivery to an audience unfamiliar with the subject may need a more logical sequence and a slower pace to allow time for detailed questions. However, those who are familiar with your subject should be able to make connections and may therefore be more interested in your reasoning and analysis.

Adapt how you engage the audience or elicit responses according to what people know. For example, an audience that is familiar with your subject is likely to reach a view and express a critical or constructive opinion fairly quickly and will expect you to justify or explain your points.

### Reading for information

As in your class work activities, you will be expected to access a range of complex and diverse material then:

- Analyse and evaluate the information it contains
- Demonstrate a sound grasp of the concepts and principles
- Synthesise them into a piece of work of your own

### Writing documents

You are expected to present a report that demonstrates intellectual depth and the ability to present complex ideas, values or views. The report should be balanced and considered; it should be free of unnecessary bias and it should present your conclusions and judgements clearly.

Check your facts are accurate, your words are well chosen and your sentences are short and clear. You may present your report in your own handwriting or process it using information technology. Whichever you choose, here are three things you should do:

- Use your key skills to improve your final document
- Produce a document that fits your assignment
- Include relevant images that complement your text

# Geography A-level

### About the syllabus

One of the aims of the Geography awards is to develop your own values and attitudes in relation to geographical issues and questions. You may find that group discussions or presentations give you an opportunity to share or test out these values and attitudes.

A-level students are also expected to synthesise geographical information in various ways and from different types of sources. Students are also expected to identify, select and collect quantitative and qualitative evidence from secondary sources of various types. Both these expectations overlap with the key skill requirement on reading and synthesising information.

Though your main opportunity for generating appropriate key skill evidence may come from your project work (internal assessment), there are other potential opportunities to consider. The project work will allow you to meet the key skill requirements that ask for an extended written document about a complex subject (including the use of an image). However, you still need to produce a different type of document for another purpose.

Once you've decided to go for the communication key skill, it's worth considering these two ideas:

- Mapping out the written work that you do for the geography course, and discussing with your teacher how best to meet the key skill evidence. The teacher can play an important role in setting the scene for discussions or presentations in geography.
- All evidence for this key skill doesn't have to come from your geography course. Your key skill portfolio can contain evidence from any qualification. Perhaps the second written document could come from another course.

## Written documents

- Each and every essay you do for the course is an opportunity to generate evidence of writing documents. Your preparation for these essays is an opportunity to generate evidence of reading and synthesising information.
- Producing good revision notes on a key topic can be considered as written work with a clear and important purpose. You will certainly have to ensure this work is well organised and written in a clear way and in a style that suits the reader – you.
- Key ideas and concepts will need to be clearly explained and the information coherently and logically organised. Having come up with a first copy of the notes, you could test them out on friends to make sure your explanations are clear. Then you'll be able to make sense of them perhaps weeks in the future

Wherever there is an opportunity for written work, there is also a chance to use your preparation as evidence of reading and synthesising.

## Project work and geography investigations

Geography may have up to 30% of the final grade determined by course work. This is most often done in the form of one large investigation. Check the course work requirements in your particular syllabus; it can generate large amounts of communication evidence and you should make the most of it.

- You could be expected to provide written work of up to 2500 words and containing maps, data, diagrams, tables or other ways of presenting geographic information. This will mean that you need to spend time thinking about the structure and organisation of this information. It will be a formal piece of course work contributing to your final grade and you need to select an appropriate style to suit the degree of formality required and the nature of the subject.
- The material will certainly have to be organised coherently; make effective use of headings, sub-headings, indentations, lists, etc., so your work has a logical structure and is clear to follow. Give it a proof-read to check the grammar, punctuation and spelling.

## Further opportunities for evidence

Research and preparation for your project work gives you an opportunity to address the requirements on reading and synthesising information. Having completed your fieldwork, you should consider sharing the results of your findings by doing a presentation. There are two reasons to consider this.

- No one will know your findings better than yourself and this might give you a little extra confidence to do the presentation.
- You may get useful information or feedback on any conclusions you make based on your findings from the audience.

This feedback will be useful in reviewing and revising your work. Presentations and any follow-up can be a useful way to test out your thoughts and get important feedback. A presentation will not only benefit your geography work, it will also give you an opportunity to generate key skill evidence.

You may want to consider establishing a small discussion group with people doing similar project work or with a group doing completely different topics (each has different benefits). This group should meet regularly and discuss progress made in the different projects. This will be a helpful way of generating evidence for the discussion aspects of the key skill, and it will provide you with a forum to resolve issues in your project work.

**What you must know**
Part 1: The Learning Curve will help you with the knowledge you need.

**What you must do**
Part 2: The Bottom Line will help you with the evidence you need.

# History A-level

### About the syllabus

The History awards encourage you to communicate knowledge and understanding about selected periods of history. The communication key skill is about communicating effectively in a range of situations. It asks you to show you can contribute to discussions, make presentations, read and synthesise information and write different types of document. Your history course will give you an opportunity to try all these things and the key skill will help you to gain confidence at doing them.

## Opportunities for evidence

The history content involved in generating communication evidence really depends on the topics you are studying. The following sections try to identify areas of history knowledge, skills and understanding that should be present in your courses regardless of the topic areas you choose. Hopefully, this will give you ideas about how to generate communication evidence regardless of the topic areas you study.

You will find there is a clear overlap between much of what you will be expected to do during your history course and in trying to meet the key skill requirements. The following activities should help you generate communications evidence relatively easily:

- Analysing, evaluating, interpreting and using historical sources of different kinds (especially good for generating evidence on reading and synthesising information).
- Using a range of historical concepts in appropriate ways when presenting a case or argument (good for generating evidence on making a presentation and writing documents).
- Using historical sources, arguments and discussions to explain, analyse and synthesise and to make judgements and draw conclusions (also good for generating evidence on reading and synthesising information).
- Doing coursework or internal assessment. In some history courses the internal assessment component can be up to 30%. This can give you an opportunity to generate extended documents about complex subjects (including at least one image). This is a main requirement of the last part of the communication key skill.

## Historical skills

### *Analysing, interpreting and evaluating sources*

This will be a key aspect of your course regardless of the period you are studying. You should use this as an opportunity to read and synthesise information. You will find that the key skill is looking to determine whether you can read extended documents, like textbooks and secondary sources, articles and reports, to identify relevant material. This could be about obtaining historical evidence or to help you understand significant events, individuals or issues. This part of your history course represents a great opportunity to address this part of the key skill, without having to do too much additional work over and above the work you need to do for the history course. It also provides you with an opportunity to scan and read material to find specific information and to find and skim read documents.

As you look at different sources of historical information you will become aware of the potential for different interpretations of topics, issues or themes and the potential for bias in interpreting sources. This is an important part of learning about what historians do and can be guilty of, and learning about how evidence can create differences of opinion and can be used to justify different interpretations of events. This type of work gives you an opportunity to address the key skill requirements on comparing accounts, recognising opinion and the potential for bias.

Any work you do with sources of historical information will give you an opportunity to generate communication evidence for:

- Using appropriate sources of reference to help you understand complex lines of reasoning and information from texts and images.
- Synthesising information you obtain for a purpose, perhaps to understand significant events or the impacts of historical developments.

### Making judgements about history and historical events

This may mean using historical sources, accounts and interpretations, then analysing them and synthesising your findings (drawing them together) to make judgements and draw conclusions. This might be an opportunity to show you can present your own interpretation of a historical event, issue or subject, bringing information together in a coherent way for an essay (or presentation).

There might even be an opportunity to share your findings and opinions as part of a discussion group. This would allow you to address this part of the key skill. Many schools and colleges may even have a history club or society that would provide further opportunities to discuss historical topics. The opinions you and others have about a historical event or issues could be debated in class, creating an opportunity to present a complicated line of reasoning or argument. For a healthy and enjoyable history discussion and to generate evidence for your key skill, besides putting across your points, you have to do three important things:

- Be receptive to the ideas of others
- Demonstrate listening skills
- Encourage others to participate

### Doing project work

Any project work you do, whether it is for personal interest or part of an internal assessment, will give you an opportunity to work with sources and to read and synthesise information. There may also be opportunities to discuss your work with other class members as part of a discussion group, using this as an opportunity to target that part of the key skill as well. You could also present your findings and conclusions, helping you to address that part of the key skill. However, perhaps the best opportunity from project work is the chance to produce an extended document about a complex subject.

You should try to use at least one image in your text to help amplify or illustrate a point made in your text. If you look carefully at the key skill requirements for writing documents, you will see that by striving to achieve them you will produce better quality history work. For example, in meeting the key skill requirements you will also be using appropriate vocabulary, sentence structures and tone to suit your intended reader and the nature of the subject. You will also be giving your work an appropriate structure and linking ideas in an appropriate way. You will have to show that you double-checked your work to spot any errors or mistakes. All this will help you develop better quality work and may help you avoid losing marks in the internal assessment.

**What you must know**
Part 1: The Learning Curve will help you with the knowledge you need.

**What you must do**
Part 2: The Bottom Line will help you with the evidence you need.

## Mathematics A-level

### About the syllabus

The Mathematics award aims to develop your understanding of mathematics and mathematical processes in a way that increases your capability

and confidence in the subject. The ability to reason logically and to generalise will help you to recognise how problems, tasks and situations can be represented mathematically and then resolved, refined or improved. You will be expected to extend your range of mathematical skills and techniques and apply them in increasingly challenging contexts as well as recognising coherence and progression across and within the subject.

Unlike other awards at this level, Mathematics A-level has no requirement for you to demonstrate the quality of your written communication. Nevertheless, it does provide you with opportunities to select and apply your communication key skill as you explore the application of mathematics to solve real problems in other fields of study or interest as well as the world of work.

## Topic area 1
## Application of Mathematics

During your programme you are required to recall, select and use your mathematical knowledge to represent real situations. You will then be expected to manipulate your mathematical expressions using appropriate graphs, sketches and diagrams to arrive at a sensible and sustainable interpretation of your results and communicate your conclusions and findings in an appropriate form.

### Discussion
Used correctly, mathematics is an effective means of communication. However, as you develop your skills you will be expected to:

- Discuss your interpretation of results with other people
- Comment constructively on other people's interpretations
- Discuss your ideas for devising mathematical models
- Consider other people's comments on your ideas
- Refine your models in the light of people's comments

### Reading for information
Mathematics uses precise language and you will be expected to read, recognise and understand the full range of mathematical facts, concepts and techniques then select and apply them to real problems. However, not all mathematics or mathematical information is presented using the signs, symbols and expressions that comprise mathematical language. Your programme requires you to:

- Read and comprehend mathematical arguments and research articles
- Synthesise the essentials of complex mathematical ideas
- Distil information then comment on its relevance to your context

### Writing documents
There is no requirement to produce extended written text as part of your programme. Nevertheless, mathematics at this level:

- Deals with complex ideas and information

- Uses appropriate styles and formats
- Requires organised information
- Makes clear use of technical words
- Explains by graphs, tables and diagrams

How much of your mathematics will count as evidence for the communication key skill will depend upon how you choose to approach your own learning in the subject, your evaluation of your mathematical development and your approach to recording and presenting your conclusions and findings.

Solving problems in applied mathematics can generate evidence in these forms:

- Records of your discussions with, or presentations to, other people on mathematics and mathematical processes.
- Notes, records or evidence of your ability to synthesise the complex ideas distilled from mathematical journals, reports or other forms of text.
- An extended document that presents your judgements, conclusions and findings plus an evaluation of your methods, models or processes along with your recommendations for the future.
- Make sure you apply the rules of grammar, punctuation and spelling.

# Physics A-level

### *About the syllabus*
The Physics awards aim to develop essential knowledge and understanding in physics and to show how physics is applied. They will also help you develop a connection between theory and experiment, an appreciation of how physics is used, and an idea of how it has developed up to now.

## Topic areas

The principles of communication occur throughout physics, especially in these five areas:

*See also:* **Science Vocational A-level**, page 123.

- Using sources of information
- Planning practical investigations
- Gathering experimental data
- Making calculations and developing data
- Presenting results and drawing conclusions

### *Discussion*
Physics investigations and experiments offer opportunities to develop and display your speaking and listening skills in various situations:

- Working with others to plan and collect observations
- Investigating equipment and procedures for using equipment
- Selecting appropriate equipment and techniques

- Agreeing safe working practices and procedures
- Investigating relevant theory and information
- Analysing data to give statistical information
- Making calculations to investigate a theory
- Testing hypotheses and making predictions
- Evaluating numerical information

Remember to show that you can participate with other people by:

- Making contributions when helpful
- Listening carefully to others
- Encouraging others to contribute

### Presentation

Projects and assignments in physics offer good opportunities to present and discuss your findings with the help of various presentation techniques which use text, images and numbers. Here are some typical opportunities:

- Explaining a topic in physics
- Presenting statistical data, trends, etc.
- Presenting calculations for theoretical work
- Presenting calculations for practical work
- Varying the values in a model
- Testing hypotheses and making predictions

### Reading for information

The processes of investigation and experimentation in physics require you to use extended documents and databases of information. Some information is from commercial sources and you need to recognise any bias as you select suitable data. You then need to assemble and use this information in the most appropriate manner for your targets. Here are some relevant activities:

- Obtaining background information from online and offline databases
- Obtaining physical data from online and offline databases
- Finding out about equipment and how to use it
- Using IT interfaces to gather data from equipment
- Selecting suitable information from experimental data
- Assembling data from database searches or practical work
- Analysing data to give statistical information such as trends
- Making calculations for practical work or theories
- Varying the values in a model
- Testing hypotheses and making predictions

### Writing documents

You need to use documents to communicate your results in an effective manner. Assignments and projects in physics offer opportunities for generating a range of documents with complex information, using specialist language and including images. The key skill requires that you choose the best form and style of writing and organise the material coherently. Here are some opportunities for evidence:

- Using graphs, charts and diagrams
- Presenting OHTs or computer slides
- Explaining scientific theories and processes
- Recording results in a laboratory notebook
- Presenting calculations and making predictions
- Printing out spreadsheets to show calculations
- Making notes before or after a discussion
- Sending memos or emails to other people

The key skill requires you to present documents that are clearly written and have accurate spelling, punctuation and grammar. Redraft your work until it reads nicely then give it a proof-read to check for mistakes. Maybe ask other people to look it over.

## Further opportunities for evidence

Most scientific investigations provide good opportunities to collect evidence for the communication key skill unit. Some applications of physics, such as nuclear energy, involve issues which feature in national and international debates, and examining them will provide further opportunities for gathering evidence.

**What you must know**
Part 1: The Learning Curve will help you with the knowledge you need.

**What you must do**
Part 2: The Bottom Line will help you with the evidence you need.

Opportunities

EVIDENCE FROM A-LEVEL COURSES | **91**

# Evidence from Vocational A-level courses

## Art and Design Vocational A-level

See also: **Art A-level**, page 62.

### About the specifications

The Art and Design award studies topics such as working with materials; developing and exploring your use of visual language; working with materials, techniques and technology; and working to set briefs. It also includes course work and personal investigations and presentation of work. Your communication key skill is built into your GNVQ. It should be seen as a central component of your work in art, craft and design and it should be used to complement your developing 2D and 3D language.

### Topic area 1
### Designing and making skills

### Discussion

When designing and making in art, craft and design you will need to consider these questions very carefully

- What am I making?
- Why am I making?it
- For whom am I making it?

Considering these questions will provide you with the ideal opportunity to develop your speaking and listening skills as you explore the media, materials, techniques and technology you will need to use. Discuss things with your tutors and other people.

Informal discussions, perhaps with your tutors or other students, will be casual and unplanned. They are likely to happen as you are working on a technique or activity that does not require your full concentration, e.g. priming a canvas. These occasions will give you the opportunity to practise and rehearse the discussion skills needed for more formal situations.

A group discussion is likely to be organised by your tutor to:

- Plan and prepare individual or group work at the start of a project
- Explore how a project is going and review schedules
- Review how a project has gone and evaluate outcomes

These occasions will enable you to demonstrate effective speaking and listening skills by:

- Knowing how and when to participate by using body language to show involvement, and thoughtful comments to show understanding.
- Listening attentively and responding appropriately by using voice and vocabulary that are consistent with the points and ideas being discussed.
- Making sure that everyone has the opportunity to participate by valuing their contributions and following up their comments with supplementary questions.

## Presentation

Presenting art, craft and design work is a natural part of creative development. You will need to be aware at all times of your purpose and your audience. Artists, craftspeople and designers have a great advantage over others during presentations because they will always have an available source of visual images or models to help them clarify or reinforce a point. Other skills may not come so easily but they need to be developed. They include:

- Organising and using your visual images to help you prepare
- Confidence in using specialist language
- Structuring your presentation to help the audience follow it
- Putting sketches or models in a chronological sequence
- Speaking clearly, confidently, slowly and with sensitivity

## Reading for information

As you gain experience in your own 2D and 3D visual language, you will be expected to explore a range of information sources on:

- Other artists, craftspeople and designers
- Alternative ways to express ideas and feelings
- New technology and equipment
- Current thinking on art, craft and design
- Innovative ways to present art, craft and design.

One thing is certain: there is no shortage of visual stimuli or literature on contemporary and historical topics in art, craft and design. To be effective at information gathering, you will need to synthesise this diverse information and use it to develop your creative skills. This will include:

- Skimming sources as you search for new ideas
- Scanning selected sources to extract information
- Checking details from one source in another
- Making judgements on new ideas and images
- Selecting items that match or challenge your intentions
- Adapting new ideas to develop your creativity

### Writing documents

This topic will provide you with the opportunity to produce extended documents such as:

- An illustrated exhibition catalogue
- An illustrated presentation
- An illustrated evaluation of a project

You may also wish to use your visual log or your sketchbooks as important sources of evidence if you believe they meet the criteria for effective written information.

## Topic area 2
## Other people's use of visual language

A central theme is an appreciation of historical and contemporary practice in art, craft and design. When seeking historical and contemporary references, as well as professional practice, you will have the opportunity to:

- Discuss your planned research with your tutor
- Share your findings with others on your programme
- Talk to artists, craftspeople and designers
- Visit libraries to seek help and advice on appropriate resources
- Attend lectures or visit museums and art galleries

At this level you should already have the skills to discuss other people's work with your peers in an informal situation. The greater challenges come when you meet unfamiliar individuals in more formal settings.

Your tutor may arrange for an artist, craftsperson or designer to visit your course to run a workshop and hold a seminar or you may have the opportunity to attend a lecture on art, craft or design organised by a gallery. These situations will provide you with an opportunity to put your oral skills to the test. If you sit and say nothing, you may regret it later.

The important thing is timing; you should know:

- When to participate or ask a question
- When to stop talking; be concise
- When to ask a supplementary question
- When you can help others to ask their questions

### Presentation

You may have the opportunity to present your research to others. This is an ideal opportunity for you to combine your understanding of art, craft and design with effective communication skills. To do this you must achieve the right balance between what you say, how you say it and what you show:

- Produce a set of visual aids such as overhead transparencies (OHTs), slides or illustrations of the work you are talking about
- Draw up a set of notes that will help you and others keep on track or to explain more detailed points such as biographical or chronological details

- Check that any technology you intend to use works, including microphones, overhead projectors or PowerPoint systems
- Be confident and comfortable with your chosen presentation
- Be aware of your audience's needs: explain any technical terms you may use, give access to any aids or handouts, make sure everyone can see and hear you
- Use the right pace and structure; sequence your images and match your words to the image on display.

### Reading for information

The amount, detail and range of sources available to you will vary according to the artist, craftsperson or designer you are studying. It may be hard to obtain information on a contemporary designer. However, a fine artists who has had a major exhibition may well be the subject of reference books, magazine articles and newspaper reviews. Typical sources include:

- Galleries, museums and private collections
- Textbooks and reference books
- Magazines and newspapers
- Catalogues and pamphlets
- Personal letters and articles
- Websites and CD-ROMs

Your biggest dilemma will not be finding sources, skimming for relevance or scanning and reading for detail, but arriving at a balanced or, more importantly, personal perspective on the work that you have investigated. This is because, no matter who you are, views are subjective in art, craft and design:

- Artists, craftspeople and designers have subjective views
- Authors, art historians and researchers have subjective views
- Critics, reviewers and commentators have subjective views
- Peoples, cultures and societies have subjective views
- You, your tutors and your peers have subjective views

As you form your own views, look at the context in which individual writers were working, because this will usually have an impact on what they say. Once you are aware of subjectivity and how it appears in opinion and bias, you can make your own decisions and synthesise the ideas, attitudes, interpretations and values accordingly.

### Writing documents

Your work on this topic should result in a portfolio of your historical and contemporary references. This investigation alone should provide you with an opportunity to generate all the evidence you need to meet the key skill requirements.

Your portfolio, whatever form it takes, should meet the first requirement to be an extended document. Other evidence can be drawn from:

- Slides, aids and handouts for your presentation
- Summaries and synthesised documents

**What you must know**
Part 1: The Learning Curve will help you with the knowledge you need.

**What you must do**
Part 2: The Bottom Line will help you with the evidence you need.

Opportunities

- Any ideas you have developed
- Memos, letters or emails you have sent

Written evidence at this level must be legible and apply the rules of grammar, punctuation and spelling.

# Business Vocational A-level

### About the specifications

The Business awards study a range of topics; the compulsory units give you a broad understanding of some fundamentals and the optional units are slightly more specialised. Both can be used to generate key skill evidence. It is worth learning a little bit about all the units you are likely to study. This will allow you to get a better idea of how you can build up your portfolio of evidence for the communication key skill, identifying which units can be used to generate evidence for the different key skill demands.

Here are some suggestions for how to use compulsory units to create key skill evidence. This information is designed to help you start planning and collecting the key skill evidence you need.

*See also:* **Business Studies A-level**, page 69; **Retail and distributive Services Vocational A-level**, page 120.

## Marketing

### Discussion

The marketing unit may require you to collect market research information using primary sources of information and secondary form of information, like market research data. Each represents a separate opportunity to share results and your interpretation of this data with a group. This will create an opportunity to meet these particular key skill requirements and give you an opportunity to focus attention on your thoughts and findings, gathering them together and trying out them out on others. This might be a useful way to prepare your ideas before you submit them as part of your final marketing strategy for the Business assessment.

### Presentation

Primary research findings and conclusions are particularly good for presentations. This is mainly because they are your findings and you will know more about them than anybody in the audience. This may give you a little more confidence when it comes to doing the presentation. Primary research data also presents you with the challenge of communicating statistics or numerical data to your audience clearly and effectively. This means learning how to use appropriate visual aids. All these considerations form a great opportunity to fully address this part of the communication requirements. Holding a question and answer session after your short presentation will also allow you to gauge other people's reactions to your conclusions and might even give you some ideas from other people. This can be used and fed back into improving your final work for the marketing strategy used in your business assessment.

### Reading for information

The ability to skim extended texts, scan material and use appropriate sources of reference (all requirements for this part of the key skill) will be useful in producing your marketing strategy generally. You could also channel this (the reading and synthesising information effort) into preparation for a topic your want to present or discuss. You will also find specialist reference material to help you come to terms with key marketing terms and concepts that you should use to make sure you have a clear understanding of what you read.

### Writing documents

You may need to produce your marketing strategy in the style of a business document. This means a formal business style of writing is necessary and the organisation and structure of your work should meet with the appropriate conventions or expectations of this type of document. This provides you with a great opportunity to show you can produce a distinct type of written document about a complex subject. You may also be able to incorporate images as well. You will certainly be addressing the key skill requirements to make sure you use a form and style of writing appropriate to your purpose (a business marketing strategy). The requirement to ensure you organise your information clearly and coherently, using specialist (marketing) vocabulary where appropriate, and the requirement to ensure your spelling, grammar and punctuation are accurate, both will increase the quality of your final work. This means your business evidence will be stronger, of better quality and may begin to meet some of the grading requirements.

## Competitive business environments

### Discussion

There are several topics that might be difficult to grasp at first. A useful way of dealing with them is to do some preparation and reading on your own then discuss the topics in a group. Come armed with points to make and questions to ask. Start with a question the group has to discuss and form some sort of conclusions about, or start with an issue that needs to be resolved. Perhaps you can get a teacher to help you with this. Giving the discussion some sort of focus makes it easier to prepare and keep moving. Here are some topics you might like to consider:

- The characteristics of a market or several different markets
- The influence of government economic policy

### Presentation

As preparation for the final business assessment, why not consider working on a case study of a UK business or a business that operates in a market heavily influenced by international competition? Use this as the focus of a presentation or discussion. You could even do one type of business for each different type of key skill requirement, e.g. one business type for discussion, the other for presentation. This will help you prepare both

individually and in a group, developing and revising the types of analytical skills that may be important in the assessment.

### More presentation

Some topics in this unit lend themselves to particular types of presentation and give you a chance to demonstrate your skills. For example, the influence of government economic policy on business is quite subjective. It really depends on your political standpoint or opinion. Therefore it should be possible to stage a presentation with a number of students who have differing opinions on the influence of the government's economic policies. This should make for an interesting, entertaining and stimulating discussion, presentation or debate.

### Reading for information

There will be several opportunities to focus on key areas of this subject that will be important for the final assessment. As you work to develop a coherent and clear set of revision notes for the assessment or prepare for a discussion or presentation, you can also pick up this part of the key skill requirements. Some topic areas, such as the influence of government economic policy on business, will be very subjective and the views of the authors you read will be influenced by their own political opinions. This might influence how they choose to ignore, dismiss or overemphasise some economic data or facts. Learning how to detect this type of bias is a useful skill to have; it is a requirement in this part of the key skill.

## Finance

Regardless of how this topic is assessed in the GNVQ, there will still be an opportunity to generate communication evidence. The suggestions for how to approach communication in this unit are really the same as for the unit on competitive business environments. Focus on topics that need particular attention when it comes to revision and use them as the focus for discussions and/or presentations. When it comes to reading and synthesising information, you will find there are specialist reference sources that can be particularly useful in helping you understand what you read.

## Business planning

### Discussion

Much like the advice given above, choosing difficult areas as the focus of discussions can be a useful way of learning from other people and helping other people to understand. Financial planning, break-even analysis, cash flow forecasting and start-up balance sheets are areas that could be discussed and explored, perhaps focusing the preparation and discussion on a real-life set of examples.

### Presentation

Sharing the findings of the primary research or secondary research and the conclusions you draw from your data can be useful ways of testing out your ideas as preparation for your final assessment. It is also a great way of meeting these key skill requirements.

### Writing documents

There might be specific conventions and expectations to meet when you produce a business plan. These may influence your organisation and style. Showing that you can meet these expectations successfully will mean that you also address important parts of the key skill requirements. Following through the other requirements in this part of communication (like grammar, punctuation, spelling, concern about the organisation and structure) may also mean that the quality of your final work improves. This may make you better prepared to meet some of the grading requirements.

**What you must know**
Part 1: The Learning Curve will help you with the knowledge you need.

**What you must do**
Part 2: The Bottom Line will help you with the evidence you need.

# Construction and the Built Environment Vocational A-level

### About the specifications

The Construction and Built Environment awards study towns and cities that make up the environment, including their buildings and the civil engineering structures that provide their infrastructure. They also include the technology and performance of structures, buildings and services within buildings, such as water supplies and energy supplies. Optional units cover architecture and design, building, civil engineering, building services engineering, town planning and development.

## Topic areas

Common to all studies in construction and the built environment are the processes of investigating, surveying, measuring, designing and reporting results. The principles of communication are relevant to all studies and may be considered under focus areas such as:

- Investigating the built environment and its impact
- Evaluations and surveys
- Design procedures
- Management of procedures and finance
- Performance of materials, structures and services.

### Discussion

Investigations in construction and the built environment offer opportunities to develop and display your speaking and listening skills in the following situations:

- Evaluating environmental issues, town features, service features and other topics needed for your investigations

EVIDENCE FROM VOCATIONAL A-LEVEL COURSES | **99**

**Opportunities**

- Working with others while planning and collecting observations and measurements
- Evaluating data on population, economy and other information about towns and regions
- Agreeing approaches to client needs and design options
- Gathering technical data, evaluating its worth and making choices based upon it

Remember to show you can participate in discussions by listening carefully, making your own contributions and encouraging other people to make theirs.

### Presentation

Projects in construction and the built environment offer good opportunities to present and discuss findings with the help of presentation techniques using text, images and numbers. Here are some typical situations:

- Presenting information about towns, structures and installations
- Presenting details of design options and final choices
- Presenting statistical data, trends and other results
- Presenting the results of energy-use calculations
- Showing details of design using drawings and other graphics

### Reading for information

The processes of design, technology, finance and management associated with town planning, structures, buildings and services require you to use extended documents and databases of information. Some information is from commercial sources and you need to recognise any bias as you select suitable data. You then need to assemble and use this information in the most appropriate manner for your targets. Here are some typical activities relevant to the key skills unit:

- Finding background information relevant to client requirements
- Selecting and interpreting on-screen maps, plans and drawings
- Using online and offline databases for materials and components
- Assembling data sets and obtaining statistical results
- Developing drawings using computer-aided design (CAD)
- Obtaining population trends and component performances
- Calculating areas and volumes, energy use and statistical measures

### Writing documents

You need to use documents to communicate your results in an effective manner. Investigations in construction and the built environment offer good opportunities for generating a range of documents with complex information, using specialist language and including images. The key skill requires that you choose the best form and style of writing and organise the material coherently. Here are some opportunities for evidence:

- Notes made before, or after a discussion
- Memos or emails sent to members of a team

- Documents about towns and structures
- Documents on construction details and service installations
- Documents explaining environmental issues and technology
- Summaries of design options and final choices
- Statistical data and trends shown on charts and graphs
- Field readings and accompanying statistical results
- Population trends, component performances, etc.
- Calculations for land, roads, buildings and components
- Volumes of earth mounds, buildings, rooms and pipes
- Calculations of energy use in buildings
- Spreadsheets to present information and calculations

The key skill requires you to present documents that are clear and have accurate spelling, punctuation and grammar. To achieve this you may need to produce several drafts for proof-reading and correction. Check things for yourself and invite other people to look over your work.

**What you must know**
Part 1: The Learning Curve will help you with the knowledge you need.

**What you must do**
Part 2: The Bottom Line will help you with the evidence you need.

# Engineering Vocational A-level

### About the specifications
The Engineering awards study the links between engineering organisations and business, finance, the economy and the environment. It also includes units that apply principles of design, materials technology, science and mathematics. Optional units cover electrical engineering, mechanical engineering, telecommunications and automotive engineering.

See also: **Design and Technology A-level**, page 75; **Manufacturing Vocational A-level**, page 114.

## Topic areas

The principles of communication occur throughout studies in engineering, especially in these areas:

- Role of engineering in the economy and environment
- Nature of engineering organisations
- Design of engineering products and services
- Making and servicing engineering products
- Performance of engineering products
- Performance of engineering services

### Discussion
Investigations in engineering offer these opportunities to develop and display your speaking and listening skills:

- Working with others to obtain observations and measurements
- Gathering information for a design brief
- Agreeing approaches to client needs and design options
- Finding manufacturers' data for practical investigations
- Investigating the functions of an organisation
- Gathering information on engineering activities

- Gathering information on commercial activities
- Gathering information on links between parts of an organisation
- Agreeing safe working practices and procedures

Remember to show you can participate in discussions by listening carefully, making your own contributions and encouraging other people to make theirs.

### Presentation

Engineering projects and assignments offer good opportunities to present and discuss your findings with the help of presentation techniques using text, images and numbers. Here are some typical opportunities:

- Explaining the structure and functions of an organisation
- Explaining links between engineering and commerce
- Showing the information flow between parts of an organisation
- Presenting details of design options and final choices
- Presenting statistical data, trends and other results
- Presenting the results of engineering calculations
- Showing design details using computer visualisations, models, etc.

### Reading for information

The processes of investigation, design and making associated with engineering products and services require you to use extended documents and databases of information. Some information is from commercial sources and you need to recognise any bias as you select suitable data. You then need to assemble and use this information in the most appropriate manner for your targets. Here are some typical activities relevant to the key skills unit:

- Finding information about the national role of engineering
- Finding background information relevant to client requirements
- Interpreting maps, plans and technical drawings in electronic formats
- Using online and offline for materials and components
- Assembling experimental data sets and obtaining statistical results
- Developing drawings using computer-aided design (CAD)
- Calculations based on multiple sets of data and techniques

### Writing documents

You need to use documents to communicate your results in an effective manner. Engineering assignments and projects offer good opportunities for generating a range of documents with complex information, using specialist language and including images. The key skill requires that you choose the best form and style of writing and organise the material coherently. Here are some opportunities for evidence:

- Notes made before or after a discussion
- Memos or emails sent to members of a team
- Graphs, charts, diagrams and CAD drawings
- Explanations of motion, energy use and other concepts

- Final design solutions presented using graphics
- Experimental results and records of investigations
- Calculations and predictions based on their outcome
- Documents on engineering and the national economy
- Reports on how engineering companies are run
- Spreadsheets to present information and calculations

The key skill requires you to present documents that are clear and have accurate spelling, punctuation and grammar. To achieve this you may need to produce several drafts for proof-reading and correction. Check things for yourself and invite other people to look over your work.

**What you must know**
Part 1: The Learning Curve will help you with the knowledge you need.

**What you must do**
Part 2: The Bottom Line will help you with the evidence you need.

# Health and Social Care Vocational A-level

### About the specifications

The health and social care awards study a range of topics; the compulsory units give you a broad understanding fundamentals and the optional units are slightly more specialised. Both can be used to generate key skill evidence. It is worth learning a little bit about all the units you are likely to study. This will allow you to get a better idea of how you can build up your portfolio of evidence for the communication key skill, identifying which units can be used to generate evidence for the different key skill demands. The information below is designed to help you start planning and collecting the key skill evidence you need.

## Opportunities for evidence

### Discussion

Many of the communication key skills are also valuable in health and social care. Look for particular opportunities to generate communication evidence and health and social care evidence simultaneously when you study units on communicating in health and social care.

The key skill is asking you to do three things:

- Listen and respond in discussion situations, being careful to consider and adapt to gender and cultural aspects, as well as to other people's feelings in general.
- Make openings to encourage others to contribute, showing that you can be supportive and encouraging as well as receptive to the contributions of others.
- Vary how and when you participate to adapt to different purposes and situations.

In health and social care, the ability to be sensitive to these types of considerations is invaluable. The vocational assessment will probably ask you

Opportunities

to show you can communicate effectively in a one-to-one interaction and in group situations, giving you plenty of opportunities to develop and rehearse these skills.

You may even be asked to demonstrate how you can promote valuing people as individuals in a discussion setting. You can do this by not only showing sensitivity but also by using the second and third requirements.

So you see there is a strong relationship between the demands of the key skill and the demands of the vocational qualification. This means you have an opportunity to work on the evidence requirements simultaneously, using the key skill to help improve your vocational work and vice versa. Make sure you are fully aware of the communication requirements before you tackle the vocational assessment on communicating in health and social care. This will help you to generate your evidence simultaneously.

Also look for opportunities to generate discussion-related evidence when you carry out research, perhaps discussing your rationale or findings with a group. In fact, any units where you have a point of view could be discussed in a group situation, allowing you to show your discussion skills.

### Presentation

Health and social care throws up many debates and discussions. Even if there are no vocational requirements to make a presentation, you may find that presenting an argument is a useful way of preparing vocational work while generating key skills evidence. You will certainly have the opportunity to use your research findings as a presentation topic. You will also find that the techniques needed to meet the key skills requirements, e.g. engaging the audience by using illustrations or varying your tone of voice, are techniques that can be used in health and social care.

### Reading for information

Whether you are doing your own research and need to review relevant research and literature, or learn about relevant legislation which affects the rights of clients and workers, you will find the communication key skills related to reading and synthesising information invaluable. Not only will you have plenty of opportunities to generate the key skill evidence, you will also improve your techniques when working on the vocational evidence, making you much more effective at dealing with information generally.

**What you must know**
Part 1: The Learning Curve will help you with the knowledge you need.

**What you must do**
Part 2: The Bottom Line will help you with the evidence you need.

### Writing documents

The health and social care course has an emphasis on written forms of evidence. This means there are several opportunities to generate key skill evidence. The communication key skills you develop will also enhance the quality of your written work. Look for opportunities to generate evidence of writing documents when you:

- Write up your research project
- Investigate systems in the body
- Report on a care organisation

# Hospitality and Catering Vocational A-level

## *About the specifications*

The Hospitality and Catering awards study a range of topics; the compulsory units give you a broad understanding of some fundamentals and the optional units are slightly more specialised. Both can be used to generate key skill evidence. It is worth learning a little bit about all the units you are likely to study. This will allow you to get a better idea of how you can build up your portfolio of evidence for the communication key skill, identifying which units can be used to generate evidence for the different key skill demands.

Here are some suggestions for how to use compulsory units to create key skill evidence. This information is designed to help you start planning and collecting the key skill evidence you need. However, there are more general opportunities as well.

## Opportunities for evidence

Much of your portfolio work and the final evidence submitted for assessment will be written work. This will be in the form of case studies, the results of investigations, reports or records of activities. Because of this emphasis on written evidence, you will be able to meet most of the writing aspects of the key skill if you consider them when you do your vocational work.

When the vocational evidence asks for a record of activities, you will need to organise your evidence coherently. This provides an opportunity to generate this part of the key skill and learning how best to organise work effectively will give you an opportunity to improve the quality of your vocational work in general.

All written work for hospitality and catering will benefit from clear writing, proof-reading and redrafting to ensure spelling, punctuation and grammar are accurate. Developing this as part of your natural writing process will allow you to generate key skill evidence.

Skills involved in skimming extended documents, looking for specific information and using appropriate sources of reference are all relevant to the investigative work you will be required to do in specific parts of your course, e.g. investigating the hospitality and catering industry.

## Topic area 1
## Purchasing, costing and control

When you are researching the purchase cycle procedures, you may need to learn about manual and computerised systems. When you are researching how costs and prices of products and services are prepared, presented, monitored and controlled, there may also be large amounts of information

LONGMAN KEY SKILLS · LEVEL 3 · COMMUNICATION

to read and understand. You will find that these all provide opportunities to generate evidence on reading and synthesising information.

Presenting the results of data you have calculated will give you an opportunity to generate key skill evidence for making a presentation and for writing documents. Purchasing, costing and control is a useful topic to focus key skill efforts on because it requires particular types of presentation skill. Information with a particular purpose and the topic can be complex. This will provide a good opportunity to match your language and style to suit the complexity of the subject and to relate the message appropriately to your audience. To keep it interesting, you will also have to use techniques to engage your audience.

When presenting the results of calculations in written documents, you will have the same issues and concerns. You will have to select appropriate forms for presenting this type of information to suit your purpose.

## Topic area 2
## Investigating aspects of the industry

| Hospitality and catering areas | Communications opportunities |
| --- | --- |
| Investigating the industry | • Your results of investigation work or projects can be written up to try to generate evidence for writing documents<br>• You could also present some aspects of this to the group, generating evidence for making a presentation<br>• Your investigations into the industry will allow you to generate evidence for reading and synthesising information |
| Food and drink operations | When presenting your evaluation of different food and drink operations, you will have the opportunity to:<br>• Discuss your results and findings, generating evidence you have taken part in discussions<br>• Generate communications evidence by presenting your evaluation to a group<br>• Writing up the evaluation will generate evidence for writing documents |
| Customer service | Once the group has collected information about customer services in different outlets, you should be able to have a discussion about your findings. This will help you generate evidence on discussions and give you an opportunity to rehearse any points you wish to make or thoughts you intend to use in your final vocational evidence |

| Accommodation and front office operations | Any work done assessing the impact of environmental and technological change on activities undertaken in this area can be either presented or written up, giving you the opportunity to generate evidence for either of these key skill areas |
| --- | --- |
| Safety, security and the environment | You might be asked to present some of your findings to a range of people using different methods of communication. If so, it is worthwhile taking time to use this as a major opportunity to generate communication evidence<br><br>You will find that by working on selecting appropriate forms of presentation, selecting appropriate styles, organising material coherently and making the meaning clear, you will not only meet the requirement on writing documents but you will also meet some of the vocational pass requirements |

**What you must know**
Part 1: The Learning Curve will help you with the knowledge you need.

**What you must do**
Part 2: The Bottom Line will help you with the evidence you need.

# Information and Communication Technology Vocational A-level

### *About the specifications*

The Information and Communication Technology awards study a range of topics; the compulsory units giving you a broad understanding of some fundamentals and the optional units are slightly more specialised. Both can be used to generate key skill evidence. It is worth learning a little bit about all the units you are likely to study. This will allow you to get a better idea of how you can build up your portfolio of evidence for the communication key skill, identifying which units can be used to generate evidence for the different key skill demands.

Here are some suggestions for how to use compulsory units to create key skill evidence. This information is designed to help you start planning and collecting the key skill evidence you need.

## Opportunities for evidence

### *Discussion*

- **IT serving organisations:** you have an opportunity to share the findings of the investigation into a suitable organisation with the group in the form of a discussion about some related IT topic. Try to

structure the discussion around some aspect of IT that will allow you (and others) to draw on the organisations you have studied to help further the discussion. This way you get a chance to try out some of your thinking on others and hear what they have to say on the topic based on their own findings. This might be useful in helping you review and improve your IT work before you submit it as evidence, as well as allowing you to generate evidence for this particular aspect of the key skill.

- **Spreadsheet design**: consider establishing a small discussion forum that meets regularly to discuss aspects of the work and the various advantages and limitations of spreadsheet technology. You could discuss how to come up with various spreadsheet solutions for different problems, talking about what the key design concerns might be. This type of forum would not only give you a chance to generate the necessary key skill evidence but would also give you a chance to revise and improve your understanding of the area.
- **Programming**: the suggestions for spreadsheets can be applied to programming too.

### Presentation

- **IT serving organisations**: the results of your own investigation into a suitable organisation can be a useful focus for a presentation. This is mainly because they are your own personal findings and thoughts, so you know the material well (better than the audience) and this may help give you a little more confidence when you come to give the presentation. The nature of the topic you discuss will also mean using visual aids to help you get your points across. As well as being a useful opportunity to generate this part of the key skill evidence, having to do a presentation on the results of your work can be a useful way of testing out your work on others before you submit it as IT evidence. This gives you a chance to get some feedback on the work and to make revisions or improvements to it.
- **Spreadsheet design**: consider presenting your final spreadsheet solution to an audience and using this as the focus for your key skill efforts to generate presenting evidence. Talk the group through your design specification, problems you encountered and how they were resolved; use examples of the work as visual aids. The advantage of using this type of content for your presentation is that you know your own work and the related thought processes very well, better than anyone else, and this may boost your confidence a little.

### Reading for information

- **General**: generally speaking, there should be several units that could be used to generate evidence for this type of activity. You could use this part of the key skill to prepare information for any discussion or presentation you do, or it could be part of the preparation process for reports that you have to write.
- **Communications and networks**: there might be a range of different

background reading and research that you need to do to prepare for this unit. If so, take this opportunity to collect evidence for this part of the key skill. Early on in the process of collecting information, look to see what can be used as examples of extended documents to work on; you will need two. The reading and synthesising could have one of two purposes: (1) to produce notes for turning into final evidence as a network specification or (2) to make research notes that help you collect your portfolio of information and software downloaded from the Web.

### Writing documents

- **Presenting information**: this topic could be used to produce both types of the written documents the key skill asks for. The first is the extended piece; it could involve describing, comparing and evaluating two different standard documents used by the organisations studied. This could present a presentational and organisational challenge as you work out how best to present it in a logical and coherent way.
- **A great opportunity**: many of the vocational requirements may well be the IT equivalent of what the communication key skill is asking you to consider. This close relationship gives you a great opportunity to meet the key skill requirements. The relationship between the two units may continue further as vocational grading requirements for IT may ask that you show evidence of proof-reading and annotations of how you achieved a coherent and consistent style and ensured your content was appropriate.
- **IT serving organisations**: when you come to write up the report for this unit, you have the opportunity to use this as a chance to generate evidence for this part of the key skill. The subject matter is certainly complex enough and the report will be an extended document. Because the vocational work will probably require you to use diagrams when describing the main functions, departments or structures of an organisation, you have plenty of opportunities to include images.
- **Communications and networks**: the specification for a computer network could be used to address one of the two different types of documents about complex subjects.

# Land and Environment Vocational A-level

### About the specifications

The Land and Environment awards study a range of topics; the compulsory units give you a broad understanding of some fundamentals and the optional units are slightly more specialised. Both types can be used to generate key skill evidence. It is worth learning a little bit about all the units

**What you must know**
Part 1: The Learning Curve will help you with the knowledge you need.

**What you must do**
Part 2: The Bottom Line will help you with the evidence you need.

**Opportunities**

you are likely to study. This will allow you to get a better idea of how you can build up your portfolio of evidence for the communication key skill, identifying which units can be used to generate evidence for the different key skill demands. The information below is designed to help you start planning and collecting the key skill evidence you need.

## Opportunities for evidence

### *Discussion*

You will find that all units can involve some degree of discussion, and most vocational work will benefit from taking time to have a formal discussion about some of the key topics. This is also a good way to revise areas that could feature in external assessments.

Remember that the key skill is trying to help you take part in discussions as an effective group member. It is asking you to prove that you have the variety of skills needed to be an effective participant. Do not approach these discussions merely as opportunities to show how much you know. You will need to demonstrate that you can make appropriate contributions (and avoid inappropriate contributions), listen to others and encourage them. Make sure you are fully aware of what the key skill is trying to assess before you actually take part in discussions. Here are some areas that may give you opportunities:

- **Monitoring and managing ecosystems**: it doesn't matter if you all discuss the same ecosystem or use ecosystems that the group have studied individually. Just make sure that you have a single issue or focus that targets some aspect of the unit. Then you can use your knowledge of the same ecosystem or of your own particular system to draw on in the discussion. Ensure that the group knows about the topic in advance and allow for sufficient preparation time.

- **A possible focus**: one possible focus is the explanation of how external factors influence your ecosystem and the evaluation of its biodiversity and sustainability. In this example you will find it useful to listen to the approach taken by others and their thoughts on the issues. This should help and encourage you to be a better listener and show that you are receptive to the approaches and ideas of others. You may also be able to learn from the others and improve or refine your own work.

- **Other topics**: you could choose to discuss the management of your local ecosystem or the animal and plant adaptations to it. You might also consider focusing your discussion on the results of a practical survey.

- **Environmental impact**: you could participate in a general discussion about the impact of a business organisation, sharing with the group your impact analysis and listening to and contributing to the analysis of others. This is particularly beneficial if you have each looked at different businesses.

- **Natural resources**: in fact, any unit that involves practical investigations allows you to use the results of your investigative work as potential topics for discussion. This particular unit also could contain an analysis of how the activities of a business impact on the landscape; this could form a useful discussion topic.

## Presentation

- **Monitoring and managing ecosystems**: you could present primary data collected on species present in an ecosystem.
- **Environmental impact**: you could take an aspect of your environmental impact analysis (e.g. explaining the ecological and visual impact of a business on the environment, including comments on the use of renewable and non-renewable resources) and make this the focus of a presentation.
- **Investigations and results**: any unit that involves practical investigation and result taking could be used as a way to generate evidence of presentation. Finding effective ways to communicate results and to keep the audience interested will help you generate appropriate evidence and help you develop useful skills. There are clear advantages of using your own research or investigation work as the subject for your presentation. Because they are your results or findings, you should know them better than anyone in the audience. This might give you a little more confidence when you make presentations. Results can also be shown using visual aids, which will help you address other aspects of the key skill.

## Reading for information

This aspect of the key skill evidence requirements can really be met using any of the units you are likely to study. You will find the skills that need to be developed in this part of the key skill invaluable in all your work. The following areas may involve more reading and researching: investigating the land and environment sector, the science of plant and animal management.

## Writing documents

This aspect of the key skill requirements really does relate to all and any written work that you are going to submit as final evidence in your land and environment portfolios. You should consider building in the key skill requirements into your general method of working when producing written work. This will help you generate key skill evidence and improve the presentation and quality of your vocational work.

The writing skills that communication can help you develop will be especially useful in land and environment, where much of your written work can involve text and charts, figures, graphs or other forms of numerical data. You may find that some units put emphasis on having a logical and well-structured approach to presenting written information. Other units may emphasise the need to present information effectively using appropriate, clear and coherent formats. There may even be times when these are mentioned as requirements for higher grades.

**What you must know**
Part 1: The Learning Curve will help you with the knowledge you need.

**What you must do**
Part 2: The Bottom Line will help you with the evidence you need.

# Leisure and Recreation Vocational A-level

## About the specifications

The Leisure and Recreation awards study a range of topics; the compulsory units give you a broad understanding of some fundamentals and the optional units are slightly more specialised. Both can be used to generate key skill evidence. It is worth learning a little bit about all the units you are likely to study. This will allow you to get a better idea of how you can build up your portfolio of evidence for the communication key skill, identifying which units can be used to generate evidence for the different key skill demands. The information below is designed to help you start planning and collecting the key skill evidence you need.

See also: **Travel and Tourism,** page 125.

## Opportunities for evidence

### Discussion

You will find that all units can involve some degree of discussion, and most vocational work will benefit from taking time to have a formal discussion about some of the key topics. This is also a good way to revise areas that could feature in external assessments.

Remember that the key skill is trying to help you take part in discussions as an effective group member. It is asking you to prove that you have the variety of skills needed to be an effective participant. Do not approach these discussions merely as opportunities to show how much you know. You will need to demonstrate that you can make appropriate contributions (and avoid inappropriate contributions), listen to others and encourage them. Make sure you are fully aware of what the key skill is trying to assess before you actually take part in discussions. Here are some areas that may give you opportunities:

- **Marketing:** even if this particular topic is designated as one to be externally assessed, you will find it beneficial to use aspects of it as a focus for discussions (or presentations). Then you will be able to revise areas you have studied and that are likely to come up in the external assessment. If you look at a particular case study, you should be able to target group discussions on SWOT and PEST analysis, marketing mixes or the results and analysis of any market research done.
- **Leisure and recreation in action:** you might be asked to produce a business plan for leisure and recreation projects, working in groups or individually. If you work in groups there will be ample opportunity to meet and discuss different aspects of the work. This will give you a chance to generate communication evidence and make effective contributions and help you develop the skills needed to participate fully in the team as you plan the work, solve problems and take the necessary decisions.

- **Keeping records:** the records you need to keep to show you participated effectively in your groups could also be adapted and used in your key skill portfolio. Though the key skill requirements on discussion will be looking for a different kind of evidence, you will find that developing the skills needed will benefit your performance in the team, making you a better team player. This will help improve the team performance generally and improve the quality of the vocational evidence.
- **Safe working practices:** using visits to local facilities as a focus, you could take part in before and after discussions on how you thought the facilities met relevant legislation, ensured a safe environment and security. You could also discuss what might feature in a risk assessment of the facilities visited.

### Presentation

- **The sports industry:** you have an opportunity to generate this type of key skill evidence by presenting the findings of your investigation into a particular sport you have chosen to study. The vocational evidence requirements for this area might be quite extensive, so you should focus your presentation on just one sport and present only certain aspects of the vocational evidence. For example, focus on just the scale and the economic importance of your sport in terms of employment, participation rates and financial contributions to the economy or focus on the mass media dimension of your vocational evidence requirements. You may even choose to link the two. Showing that you understand the links may well be a grading requirement.
- **Investigating leisure and recreation:** you could select an aspect of the vocational evidence that may be of particular interest to you. For example, you could identify a job that interests you, describing the personal and technical skills needed and explaining why this type of job is suited to you. This could be a good presentational challenge because it is primarily about you and may not be of much interest to others. So you will have to adapt your style and techniques to hold the audience's interest.

### Reading for information

This aspect of the key skill evidence requirements can really be met using any of the units you are likely to study. You will find the skills that need to be developed in this part of the key skill invaluable in all your work. The following areas may involve more reading and researching: marketing, the sports industry, investigating leisure and recreation.

### Writing documents

This aspect of the key skill requirements really does relate to all and any written work that you are going to submit as final evidence in your portfolios. You should consider building in the key skill requirements to your general method of working when producing written work. This will help you generate key skill evidence and improve the presentation and quality of your vocational work.

**What you must know**
Part 1: The Learning Curve will help you with the knowledge you need.

**What you must do**
Part 2: The Bottom Line will help you with the evidence you need.

# Manufacturing Vocational A-level

### About the specifications

The Manufacturing awards study a range of topics; the compulsory units give you a broad understanding of some fundamentals and the optional units are slightly more specialised. Both can be used to generate key skill evidence. It is worth learning a little bit about all the units you are likely to study. This will allow you to get a better idea of how you can build up your portfolio of evidence for the communication key skill, identifying which units can be used to generate evidence for the different key skill demands.

Here are some suggestions for how to use compulsory units to create key skill evidence. This information is designed to help you start planning and collecting the key skill evidence you need. However, there are more general opportunities as well.

See also: **Design and Technology A-level**, page 75.

## Opportunities for evidence

### Discussion

You will find that all units can involve some degree of discussion, and most vocational work will benefit from taking time to have a formal discussion about some of the key topics. This is also a good way to revise areas that could feature in external assessments.

Remember that the key skill is trying to help you take part in discussions as an effective group member. It is asking you to prove that you have the variety of skills needed to be an effective participant. Do not approach these discussions merely as opportunities to show how much you know. You will need to demonstrate that you can make appropriate contributions (and avoid inappropriate contributions), listen to others and encourage them. Make sure you are fully aware of what the key skill is trying to assess before you actually take part in discussions. Here are some areas that may give you opportunities:

- **Production planning and costing**: a good example is critical path analysis. As you look to break down the whole manufacturing and production process into an ordered sequence of simple activities (the critical path analysis), you will find great benefit in discussing this process with others. This will give you an opportunity to try out your thoughts and ideas on others and to listen to how others in the group will tackle the same problem.
- **Focuses for discussion**: there are several areas that could be the focus of discussion in a topic like production planning and costing. Make sure your discussions occur when you (and others) have learnt about the topic to be discussed or have attempted part of the assessment. You will get more out of it that way.
- **Manufacturing products**: this will be a particularly useful opportunity

to generate key skill evidence because your vocational unit requirements will probably ask you to work in teams and produce evidence of team meetings. You should consider using your team meetings as opportunities to generate evidence of discussions. You will find that meeting the key skill requirements will also make you a more effective team player and improve the quality of your vocational work overall.

- **Focus on topics**: look for opportunities to generate evidence by focusing some of the team meetings on particular topics like production planning and risk assessment. Having a common focus will help the team meetings and improve your ability to participate effectively in the discussion.
- **Quality assurance and control**: it is a good idea to look at examples from existing manufacturing industry and make them the focus of a discussion. This area may be new to you, and being able to discuss it in a group is a useful way of revising.
- **Product design**: whether your are part of a design team or working individually, there will still be opportunities to generate evidence of discussion. You could focus on the results of market research, the client brief or even your own design ideas, but try to focus on one particular aspect each time you have a discussion and let people know in advance. This will help to ensure everyone is prepared.

### Presentation
- **Product design and creation**: the unit will probably ask you to show that you can present your design proposals clearly, using appropriate techniques. Whether your intend to submit written evidence or to give a presentation, you will still be able to use this as an opportunity to generate key skill evidence. If your work is in written form, look at the requirements on writing documents. If your work is a presentation, look at the requirements on giving presentations. This will help you give a far more effective presentation. Your design presentation should give you an opportunity to meet all the requirements of this particular aspect of the key skill.
- **The world of manufacturing**: consider presenting any diagrams or graphics to a group, e.g. schematic layouts and block diagrams. You will find that the diagrams can become a useful focus for a much wider presentation based on a local organisation.
- **Health, safety and the environment**: use Sankey diagrams, systems diagrams and flow charts.

### Reading for information
This aspect of the key skill evidence requirements can really be met using any of the units you are likely to study. You will find the skills that need to be developed in this part of the key skill invaluable in all your work. The following areas may involve more reading and researching: the world of manufacturing, health and safety, environmental impact, production planning and costing.

**What you must know**
Part 1: The Learning Curve will help you with the knowledge you need.

**What you must do**
Part 2: The Bottom Line will help you with the evidence you need.

Opportunities

### Writing documents

This aspect of the key skill requirements really does relate to all and any written work that you are going to submit as final evidence in your portfolios. You should consider building in the key skill requirements into your general method of working when producing written work. This will help you generate key skill evidence and improve the presentation and quality of your vocational work.

# Media: Production and Communication Vocational A-level

### About the specifications

The Media awards study a range of topics; the compulsory units give you a broad understanding of some fundamentals and the optional units are slightly more specialised. Both can be used to generate key skill evidence. It is worth learning a little bit about all the units you are likely to study. This will allow you to get a better idea of how you can build up your portfolio of evidence for the communication key skill, identifying which units can be used to generate evidence for the different key skill demands.

Here are some suggestions for how to use compulsory units to create key skill evidence. This information is designed to help you start planning and collecting the key skill evidence you need.

## Opportunities for evidence

### Discussion

- **Producing a media product:** you have an opportunity to generate evidence for the discussion part of the key skill when you come to review the media product you helped create in terms of its technical and aesthetic quality. Each member of the discussion group may have a different perspective on the product and the production process based on the different roles played in the process. This should make for a good discussion.
- **Marketing:** you should consider using the results of your primary and secondary research as a topic for discussion, showing how they supported the marketing decisions you made. Each member could share their results with the rest of the group and the conclusions they have drawn. You may find that you can gain valuable information from others by sharing your thoughts and looking to see what the group thinks about them. You may get comments that will be useful in helping you refine or improve your work. This will be a useful way of preparing your work before you submit it as final media evidence.
- **Media industries:** this unit is likely to contain a number of topics that can be used as the focus for discussions. You will also find that

selecting a particular topic and having people prepare to take part in a discussion about it is a useful way of checking and improving your notes and revising the topic. Consider using discussions as a useful way to revise topics as a group while you also generate key skill evidence. Focus on a specific aspect of media industries rather than take on too much to discuss. This will make it easier to prepare for the discussion and to participate and keep things moving. The best discussion topics often come from something that the group needs to reach a conclusion on, or an issue that needs to be resolved.

## Presentation

- **Producing a media product**: the vocational requirements may well ask you to present the finished media product to an audience. This provides you will a good opportunity to address this part of the key skill requirements, though there are a few issues that you need to consider. The first and most important is ensuring that you fully address the key skill requirements as an individual. A joint presentation might make this more difficult. You then need to consider how best to present the product without the product itself becoming the presentation. Remember that there are some clear skills and abilities you need to show in the presentation in order for you to meet the key skill demands.

- **Marketing**: primary and secondary research findings and the conclusions you draw from them can be useful as topics to present to groups for two reasons. You know the content of your own research better than anyone and this may give you a little more confidence when you make the presentation. Secondly, you may find that in question and answer sessions, or discussion sessions after your presentation, you get useful information and feedback on the conclusions you made about your research and how you intend to take them forward in your proposed marketing strategy. This feedback could be valuable in helping you improve your work.

- **Media industries**: selecting a particular topic to present from this type of unit is a useful way of preparing or revising for unit assessment. While the discussion session allows you to revise in a group situation, the presentation can be a useful way of having you prepare and revise an area of the unit individually. Preparing for the presentation will mean making sure your notes are in order and that you have a good understanding of the specific topic you want to discuss.

## Reading for information

- **Research for media production**: this particular media unit is probably the best chance to address the requirements for this part of the key skill in full. Your purpose for reading and synthesising information would be to allow you to eventually produce a proposal for a media artefact. This is why you need to synthesise the information you read. You are likely to come across documents that include images (as required in the key skill) because of the extent of the research you

will have to do. Once you have established your topic and begin to assemble your sources of information, take time to select which two extended documents you will use as the focus for gathering your key skill evidence.

- **Marketing:** the emphasis on using secondary sources of information in the marketing unit gives you the opportunity to use this as a way to collect evidence for this aspect of the key skill. You will find extended documents to read and marketing reference sources to refer to if you get into difficulty understanding what is being said, and you will certainly have to present your own interpretation of the information you read.

- **Producing a media product:** this type of topic will require some research as you learn about your specific role in the production process. You will find you will produce better and more thorough notes to help you get a clearer idea of your role by combing the key skill requirements for this section with your research work. This will allow you to set yourself clear objectives for your role based on this research. This means that the key skill can help you collect and improve the quality of some of your vocational evidence.

**What you must know**
Part 1: The Learning Curve will help you with the knowledge you need.

**What you must do**
Part 2: The Bottom Line will help you with the evidence you need.

### Writing documents

- **Marketing:** the evidence for this type of unit is likely to be the production of a marketing strategy or report for a media product. This could be your opportunity to generate an extended document, including an image, about a complex subject. Producing written work of this type will mean selecting a suitable form and style of writing and you will also need to show you can organise your information clearly and coherently. You will also have the opportunity to show you can use specialist language coherently, and the required checks on grammar, punctuation and spelling will also benefit the overall quality of your vocational work.

# Performing Arts Vocational A-level

### About the specifications

The Performing Arts awards study a range of topics; the compulsory units give you a broad understanding of some fundamentals and the optional units are slightly more specialised. Both can be used to generate key skill evidence. It is worth learning a little bit about all the units you are likely to study. This will allow you to get a better idea of how you can build up your portfolio of evidence for the communication key skill, identifying which units can be used to generate evidence for the different key skill demands.

Here are some suggestions for how to use compulsory units to create key skill evidence. This information is designed to help you start planning and collecting the key skill evidence you need. However, there are more general opportunities as well.

## Opportunities for evidence

### *Discussion*

You will find that all units can involve some degree of discussion, and most vocational work will benefit from taking time to have a formal discussion about some of the key topics. This is also a good way to revise areas that could feature in external assessments. In any case, communication skills will help you to become effective in the performing arts sector.

Remember that the key skill is trying to help you take part in discussions as an effective group member. It is asking you to prove that you have the variety of skills needed to be an effective participant. Do not approach these discussion merely as opportunities to show how much you know. You will need to demonstrate that you can make appropriate contributions (and avoid inappropriate contributions), listen to others and encourage them. Make sure you are fully aware of what the key skill is trying to assess before you actually take part in discussions. Here are some areas that may give you opportunities:

- **Historical and contemporary contexts**: you could base a discussion around the meaning and form of any pieces you have chosen to research, or you could discuss the results of the research undertaken. You could even do both. Remember to keep your contributions focused and avoid turning them into a mini presentation. This will give you an opportunity to share your work with others and to listen and learn from their approaches.
- **Performing work**: this could be an opportunity to take the normal processes of planning, decision making and problem solving when putting on a performance, and combine them with some of the requirements of the key skill. You will find that the key requirements will also help you become a more effective group member and participant in your vocational work.

### *Presentation*

This should be an area that you will develop confidence and competence in as part of your vocational work. The key skill provides you with a chance to get additional credit and acknowledgement for the skills you are developing, and it can also help to support the vocational dimension of your work, reinforcing your development into an effective oral communicator. Look for good opportunities to generate this type of evidence in the following areas:

- **Historical and contemporary contexts**: as with discussions, you could base a presentation around the meaning and form of pieces you have researched or you could present the results of your research.
- **Creating work for a project**: when you create an appropriate outline for a project, identifying its style, structure and content, you could try

pitching it to a group in the form of a presentation. This will involve using a particular style of language and enthusiastic manner.

- **Investigating performing arts industries:** this topic or a similar one may have been chosen for external assessment. Then you might find that presenting some aspect is a useful way of studying for an external assessment, making sure you have covered a particular area and generating key skill evidence at the same time.

### Reading for information

This aspect of the key skill evidence requirements can really be met using any of the units you are likely to study where research is involved. The following areas may involve more reading and research: investigating performing arts industries, looking at historical and contemporary contexts. Articles, reviews and critiques may help you investigate historical and contemporary contexts. You should have plenty of opportunities to show you can recognise an opinion.

### Writing documents

**What you must know**
Part 1: The Learning Curve will help you with the knowledge you need.

**What you must do**
Part 2: The Bottom Line will help you with the evidence you need.

This aspect of the key skill requirements really does relate to all and any written work that you are going to submit as final evidence in your performing arts portfolios. You should consider building in the key skill requirements to your general method of working when producing written work. This will help you generate key skill evidence and improve the presentation and quality of your vocational work. However, because much of your performing arts evidence may be in forms other than written work, pay particular attention to any writing that you do produce; use it as an opportunity to generate evidence for this aspect of the key skill. For example, studying historical and contemporary contexts may lead to a written report.

# Retail and Distributive Services Vocational A-level

### About the specifications

The Retail awards study a range of topics; the compulsory units give you a broad understanding of some fundamentals and the optional units are slightly more specialised. Both can be used to generate key skill evidence. It is worth learning a little bit about all the units you are likely to study. This will allow you to get a better idea of how you can build up your portfolio of evidence for the communication key skill, identifying which units can be used to generate evidence for the different key skill demands.

Here are some suggestions for how to use compulsory units to create key skill evidence. This information is designed to help you start planning and collecting the key skill evidence you need.

# Opportunities for evidence

## Discussion

- **Finance:** you can reinforce your understanding of key areas of this unit by making them the subject of discussions. This can be a useful way of learning or revising as a group and gives you a chance to hear what others think or know about the topic. It can also be a useful way of rehearsing and revising your understanding of a subject before you submit the final vocational evidence, giving you time to revise or improve your work before you hand it in. This means you can use the opportunity to generate key skill evidence to benefit and improve the quality of your vocational work.

- **Marketing:** you could use SWOT and PEST as the focus of a discussion. This approach has two main benefits. You can take time to learn about both things and prepare for the discussion, and you can test and improve your understanding of both concepts in the group situation, learning from others and helping others to learn. This type of activity might be useful preparation for the Retail assessment as well as helping you to meet the key skill requirements.

- **Quality assurance and customer care:** topics like quality assurance can be a little hard to grasp when you first come across them. The unit may require you to investigate the customer care and quality assurance of different organisations, and this will provide you with a real opportunity to generate key skill evidence and improve your understanding of the area. Consider setting up a discussion group that will take a before and after look at the organisations you are to investigate. In the 'before' session discuss what you would expect to see in terms of customer care and quality assurance; in the 'after' session focus on what you actually saw. Even if you are all looking at different organisations, each discussion gives you the opportunity to test your understanding and to improve the quality of your retail work as well as generating key skills evidence.

## Presentation

- **Merchandising:** this unit provides a great opportunity to generate evidence for the presenting part of the key skill. You may even find that some sort of presentation is also a vocational requirement. In order to help people understand merchandising strategies within organisations, you will need to use sketches, diagrams or photography, each of which can be effective visual aids in presentations.

- **Developments in the industry:** consider using an area of this unit as a topic for discussion. Make sure it is an idea or concept that can be presented in a brief and coherent talk and could involve the use of visual aids. Topics could really involve anything from the growth of e-commerce to consumer behaviour or UK economic trends in a certain sector area. This gives you an opportunity to generate evidence for the key skill while really getting to know an aspect of the

*See also:* **Business Studies A-level**, page 69; **Business Vocational A-level**, page 96.

**Opportunities**

course. This second point will help you when it comes to producing your vocational evidence.

- **Marketing**: secondary data used to show the markets an organisation operates in could be used as the subject of a presentation. This type of topic has the advantage of being one that you will know a lot about (because it is your research) and you could use it to explain how you were able to establish important market information as a result of your research. You may feel a little more confident when presenting this type of information because you found it, know it well (probably much better than many of the audience) and have had plenty of time to work with it. The data may also provide an opportunity to use visual aids of some sort to help you get key information across to the audience. If you hold a brief question and answer session at the end of your presentation, you may find that you are able to get some important feedback on your data and ideas that will be useful in helping you revise your work and prepare for your final retail assessment.

### Reading for information

- **Finance**: two topics that might be useful to focus on for this part of the key skill are the techniques used for budgeting, forecasting and costing, and the impact of legislation on the financial administration of any organisation you study. Both might be a little hard to grasp at first. Take time to check your understanding of what is being said and consider trying to meet the key skill requirements as you learn about these areas. This is because much of what you will have to do to produce the vocational evidence reflects what the key skill requires.
- **Developments in the industry**: this unit represents a good opportunity to collect most of the evidence you require for this part of the key skill. This is because there might be a lot of reading and research to do as you try to meet the vocational requirements. Try not to get bogged down in too much information as you collect evidence. Pick an aspect of the course, perhaps one that might be contentious or cause disagreement among writers, and use this as your key skill focus. Your choice could be anything that is likely to have been written about and that causes debate. For example, the reasons for changes in the sector in your area or how economic trends have affected the sector. Having chosen a topic, look for two extended documents about it as you collect your information. The key skill asks you to show you can use documents that include images. You will probably find charts, diagrams or graphs that show changes of some sort, so you should have that covered. The nature of the unit means you are likely to be reading about a complex issue, so there is no need to worry too much about that requirement.

### Writing documents

Most of the retail vocational evidence requirements finish with some sort of report or other type of written evidence. In many cases the evidence to

**What you must know**
Part 1: The Learning Curve will help you with the knowledge you need.

**What you must do**
Part 2: The Bottom Line will help you with the evidence you need.

be submitted must reflect the nature of its purpose and be presented accordingly, e.g. in finance and marketing. This helps with the key skill requirements to meet different purposes. Other instances require a more extended piece of writing on a complex subject. For example, more lengthy work is required on retailing developments, human resources, quality assurance and customer care. Retailing provides sufficient opportunities to meet the key skills requirements for this aspect of communication.

# Science Vocational A-level

### About the specifications
The Science awards investigate the types of science, organisations and people involved in the workplace and examine their links with the community and the economy. They also include units that increase your knowledge of particular scientific areas by carrying out practical investigations and linking the results to relevant industrial processes. Some units allow you to make extended scientific investigations into chosen areas of science or aspects of the scientific workplace.

## Topic areas

The principles of communication occur throughout scientific studies, especially in these five areas:

- Investigating the scientific workplace
- Monitoring the activity of the human body
- Controlling chemical processes
- Controlling the transfer of energy
- Synthesising organic and biochemical compounds

See also: **Biology A-level**, page 66; **Chemistry A-level**, page 72; **Physics A-level**, page 89.

### Discussion
Scientific investigations and experiments offer opportunities to develop and display your speaking and listening skills in the following situations:

- Working with others to plan and collect observations
- Agreeing safe working practices and procedures
- Investigating science-based companies
- Investigating science and the community
- Investigating health norms for individuals
- Investigating indicators of physiological status
- Finding data about energy use in systems
- Finding data related to chemical processes
- Obtaining data from manufacturers and suppliers

Remember to show you can participate in discussions by listening carefully, making your own contributions and encouraging other people to make theirs.

Opportunities

### Presentation

Scientific projects and assignments offer good opportunities to present and discuss your findings using text, images and numbers. Here are some typical opportunities:

- Information about local organisations, their work and their structures
- Risk assessments for applications in industry or the environment
- Charts and graphs to present statistical data, trends and other results
- Rates of reaction, equilibrium constants and enthalpy changes
- Features of a system and its energy transfer mechanisms
- Structures and nomenclature to describe chemical compounds
- Background knowledge such as chemical and biochemical principles

### Reading for information

The processes of scientific investigation and experiment require you to use extended documents and databases of information. Some information is from commercial sources and you need to recognise any bias as you select suitable data. You then need to assemble and use this information in the most appropriate manner for your targets. Here are some relevant activities:

- Finding information about science-based companies
- Finding and selecting indicators of physiological status
- Finding and interpreting data about energy use in systems
- Finding and interpreting data related to chemical processes
- Selecting information from your own readings and surveys
- Assembling data sets and obtaining statistical results
- Using online and offline databases for materials and components
- Taking experimental readings and generating statistical results
- Making calculations based on multiple sets of data and techniques

### Writing documents

You need to use documents to communicate your results in an effective manner. Science assignments and projects offer opportunities for generating a range of documents with complex information, using specialist language and including images. The key skill requires that you choose the best form and style of writing and organise the material coherently. Here are some opportunities for evidence.

**What you must know**
Part 1: The Learning Curve will help you with the knowledge you need.

**What you must do**
Part 2: The Bottom Line will help you with the evidence you need.

- Using graphs, charts and diagrams
- Presenting OHTs or computer slides
- Explaining scientific theories and processes
- Recording results in a laboratory notebook
- Presenting calculations and making predictions
- Printing out spreadsheets to show calculations
- Making notes before or after a discussion
- Sending memos or emails to other people

The key skill requires you to present documents that are clearly written and have accurate spelling, punctuation and grammar. Redraft your work until it reads nicely then give it a proof-read to check for mistakes. Maybe ask other people to look it over.

## Further opportunities for evidence

Most scientific investigations provide good opportunities to collect evidence for the communication key skill unit. Some scientific techniques involve issues which feature in national and international debates, and examining them will provide further opportunities for gathering evidence.

# Travel and Tourism Vocational A-level

### *About the specifications*

The Travel and Tourism awards study a range of topics; the compulsory units give you a broad understanding of some fundamentals and the optional units are slightly more specialised. Both can be used to generate key skill evidence. It is worth learning a little bit about all the units you are likely to study. This will allow you to get a better idea of how you can build up your portfolio of evidence for the communication key skill, identifying which units can be used to generate evidence for the different key skill demands. The information below is designed to help you start planning and collecting the key skill evidence you need.

## Opportunities for evidence

### *Discussion*

You will find that all units can involve some degree of discussion and most vocational work will benefit from taking time to have a formal discussion about some of the key topics. This is also a good way to revise areas that could feature in external assessments.

Remember that the key skill is trying to help you take part in discussions as an effective group member. It is asking you to prove that you have the variety of skills needed to be an effective participant. Do not approach these discussions merely as opportunities to show how much you know. You will need to demonstrate that you can make appropriate contributions (and avoid inappropriate contributions), listen to others and encourage them. Make sure you are fully aware of what the key skill is trying to assess before you actually take part in discussions. Here are some areas that may give you opportunities:

- **Marketing**: even if this topic is designated for external assessment, you can still use aspects as a focus for discussions (or presentations). This will enable you to revise areas you have learned and studied that are likely to come up in the external assessment. If you look at a particular case study, you should be able to target group discussions

See also: **Leisure and Recreation Vocational A-level**, page 112.

Opportunities

on SWOT and PEST, marketing mixes or the results and analysis of any market research.

- **Travel and tourism in action**: you might be asked to produce a business plan for projects, working in groups or individually. If you work in groups, there will be ample opportunity to meet and discuss different aspects of the work. This will give you a chance to generate communication evidence and make effective contributions and help you develop the skills needed to participate fully in the team as you plan the work, solve problems and take the necessary decisions.

- **Adapt your records**: the records you need to keep to show you participated effectively in your groups could also be adapted and used in your key skill portfolio. Though the key skill requirements on discussion will be looking for a different kind of evidence, you will find that developing the skills needed will benefit your performance in the team, making you a better team player. This will help to improve the team's performance and the quality of your vocational evidence.

- **Tourist development**: there are topics in this area that you could discuss in groups as a way of preparing for assessment and to generate key skill evidence. One particularly interesting topic is the positive and negative impacts of tourism.

- **Customer service in travel and tourism**: using visits to local facilities as a focus, you could take part in before and after discussions on how you thought the facilities met their quality criteria, then evaluate the effectiveness of the customer service delivery. Discussion could try to agree on the key quality criteria for customer service, how they could be monitored and how they could be judged effective.

### *Presentation*

- **Worldwide travel destinations**: you have an opportunity to generate this type of key skill evidence by presenting to a group the findings of your investigation into a particular destination you have chosen to study. The vocational evidence requirements for this area might be quite extensive, so you should focus your presentation on just one destination and present only certain aspects of the vocational evidence. For example, focus on the importance of each destination in terms of how many UK tourists it attracts and why it attracts them. Make effective use of statistics and attempt to analyse the destination's appeal.

- **Tourism development**: you could choose an aspect of UK (or overseas) tourism likely to be important in the assessment of the unit and use this as the focus of your presentation.

- **Investigating travel and tourism**: you could select an aspect of the vocational evidence that may be of particular interest to you. For example, you could identify a job that interests you, describing the personal and technical skills needed and explaining why this type of job is suited to you. This could be a good presentational challenge because it is primarily about you and may not be of much interest to others. So you will have to adapt your style and techniques to hold the audience's interest.

### Reading for information

This aspect of the key skill evidence requirements can really be met using any of the units you are likely to study. You will find the skills that need to be developed in this part of the key skill invaluable in all your work. The following areas may involve more reading and researching: marketing, worldwide travel destinations, tourism development, investigating travel and tourism.

### Writing documents

This aspect of the key skill requirements really does relate to all and any written work that you are going to submit as final evidence in your portfolios. You should consider building in the key skill requirements to your general method of working when producing written work. This will help you generate key skill evidence and improve the presentation and quality of your vocational work.

# Index